Hearts & Rockets

LOVING HARD AND SHOOTING FOR THE STARS

*A Devotional For Teens & Young Adults Because
Growing Up Is Hard and God Is Good*

Ainsley B.

WESTBOW
P R E S S®
A DIVISION OF THOMAS NELSON
& ZONDERVAN

WestBow Press books may be ordered through booksellers or by contacting:

WestBow Press
A Division of Thomas Nelson & Zondervan
1663 Liberty Drive
Bloomington, IN 47403
www.westbowpress.com
1 (866) 928-1240

ISBN: 978-1-5127-4352-4 (sc)
ISBN: 978-1-5127-4353-1 (hc)
ISBN: 978-1-5127-4351-7 (e)

Library of Congress Control Number: 2016908208

Print information available on the last page.

WestBow Press rev. date: 6/7/2016

Dedication

Dedicated to my little sisters, Eva and Gracie.
And to all of my sisters reading this. AKA: YOU.

Also dedicated to Poppa, who always encouraged me
to work hard and do what makes me happy.
Rest in peace, Hurricane.
You'll always be "The Standard" of a man.

Acknowledgements

Thank you:

Mom and Grandmother: Thank you all for believing in me, inspiring me, and loving me through every trial, goal, and accomplishment. You've taught me to believe in my dreams, pray always, and achieve my goals and purpose.

Dad: Thanks for sharing adventures and laughter with me as well. I can count on you for a "realistic" point of view and a diet peach Snapple!

Charlie: Thank you for always stepping up and stepping in with a heart made of pure gold.

INTRODUCTION

There was nothing wrong with my life when I decided to move to Nashville. I had an amazing place to live in Baton Rouge and while I was in school there for one year, I found myself with a phenomenal group of friends. Overall, I was excited to be free from home and a freshman in college!

In my pursuit of a career in acting, I registered in an expo for acting, singing, and dancing. Dancing I don't do, but I was interested in the acting portion of the expo and had been songwriting with a friend so I figured it'd be good experience to be on stage. My mom, grandmother, and I found ourselves in Dallas, Texas, as I prepared for various events, classes, and workshops. I also began praying about whether or not I should move to Los Angeles or stay in Baton Rouge to pursue acting. Note that only two cities were in my prayer. I prayed with expectation and asked that the Lord reveal to me that week where I would need to move. I'd been dreaming of moving to Los Angeles since I was fifteen, maybe younger. If I had control over my life, I would've left during my junior year of high school and finished high school with a TV set teacher. Thank goodness I don't control my life!

After I performed a monologue I had written called "Dreamer" and after singing some Christian hymn I can't even remember because I was so nervous, as well as an original titled "I Will," I deserved an ice cream break. My friend, Bo, lived in Dallas and offered to pick me up for an ice cream run. But, right before that, we had gotten a notification that our call-backs were posted. So, this means that if any scout that was at expo wanted to give us an offer, speak with us, or just ask more questions, we were about to find out. Remember how I went for acting? HA. I got ONE acting call back and FOUR singing call backs! Three of the four were from

Nashville and though I never thought singing would be in my future, I did think acting and singing often went hand in hand, so I needed to be skilled at both. I had been to Nashville two weeks prior to the expo because one my friends lived there and I went to visit and finish up writing "I Will" for expo. So back to Bo picking me up to get ice cream. As we sat down at Sonic (where their "Blasts" will always be a guilty pleasure of mine), I was explaining to Bo my confusion concerning the callbacks, cities, and prayer when over the loud speakers I heard a song, "It's like I know where I need to be, but I can't figure out, I can't figure out. Hey now this is my desire, consume me like a fire 'cuz I just want something beautiful …" (NeedToBreathe incase you live under a rock) It hit me like a lightning bolt. I'm moving to Nashville.

After discussing, planning, and the approval of my family, I set out for Music City. For the next five years, I blogged, journaled, grew, and went through a ton of changes and lessons. I mean, a ton. Here is where you'll read about them and some of what I learned. My first year in Nashville was the hardest and most rewarding year of my life to date. I was lonely and spent a lot of time with Jesus. I had to sift through my insecurities and completely rely on the Lord. It was brutal and beautiful.

As I reflect on my time in Nashville, as I gear up for my next move, New York City, I can't help but be so humbled and thankful that the Lord has done so much work in my life. I've made lifelong friends, learned more lessons than I can even count, and every now and then, opened my heart and life up to girls who may be going through similar situations or just may need a word of encouragement. I hope that's what this is for you. I pray you will read exactly what the Lord has for you every time you open this book, and I pray your heart is ever strengthened with His love and joy. You are so loved and so worthy and so wonderful. Thank you for taking the time to curl up with part of my story. I'm praying a blessing over you, Reader. I dearly love and appreciate you.

Hearts & Rockets,
Ainsley B.

YOU & GOD

Uncomfortable

I don't know who will choose to read this and who won't. I don't know what God is doing in your life, but I know what He is doing in mine. I want you, whoever you are, to see my weaknesses. I hide tears and hurt, but I want you to see me weak and desperate for God's loving arms to wrap around me. I want Him to hold me because I'm so broken.

I recently moved to Nashville, and this move is tough. This move is really uncomfortable for me, but even more uncomfortable is publicly saying that my heart hurts. I know everyone has struggles, and I know God has called me to be uncomfortable. Listen to Kari Jobe's song, "You Are for Me," and believe the words.

I encourage you to pray and listen to God. God is for us. In this broken moment in my life, I know He is for me. It's an overwhelming feeling to know the God of the universe is my Father, and He loves me so much. I mess up, and I feel lonely and frustrated sometimes, but *He is for me. He is for you.* He won't forsake us in our weaknesses. This song reminds me that I'm okay. It encourages me to continue on this journey God has called me to and trust in Him. He has everything in control, and everything is according to His plan, not mine. Although my tears show so many different emotions, joy overcomes all of them because I hear God whispering, "I love you, daughter. I'm here."

Thank You, Jesus, for Your love and Your comfort in my uncomfortable situation. Let me lean on You and only You for direction and guidance in this time of weakness and hopelessness (Psalm 146:1).

Change

Lately, a ton of my friends have been going through some kind of change. I have too in so many ways. Change is so good when it's under God's hand and according to His plan. I wanted to write a little encouragement, if you are going through some changes. Change is tough, and it wears you out sometimes, but it's going to be okay. God will reveal His plan and purpose to you in time. Trust Him. He is there for you to seek and lean on.

I know there are so many more lessons to come. I'm excited and nervous about the thought of each one, but I know they will be amazing in the end. For those of you who may be going through change, embrace this time in your life. Enjoy the new adventure God has given you. I know what it's like to have your world uprooted and to be planted somewhere else. I won't say it's easy, but it is going to be okay, and it is worth it.

Thank You for Your guidance and love, Jesus. Thank You for going before me and planning the path before me. I pray for strength and sustainability during this season of change. I know You have the best for me, and I'm so excited to see what's next! (Jeremiah 29:11).

Isaiah 41:10

Fear not, for I am with you; be not dismayed, for I am your God. I will strengthen you. Yes, I will help you. I will uphold you with My righteous right hand.

—Isaiah 41:10

I have a shoebox by my bed filled with verses on slips of paper. Each morning I draw out a verse and think about that verse throughout the day. This morning it was Isaiah 41:10. After I've had an extremely tough day, it is difficult to keep that verse in mind. But I look up at the stars, and there's no doubt in my mind that the Word is truth. When things are tough, and I feel like I can't see the light at the end of the tunnel, I read this verse. It's so powerful that I can't possibly think of anything but staying confident in my Father. There's a reason for everything, and right now the reason for the bad times is for me to lean on Him and trust Him throughout everything. I have to be consistent in trusting God and knowing that He will never forsake me or leave me. I will not fear or be dismayed. He will protect me.

Lord, thank You for Your love and mercy and protection over me. I can do nothing without You. I would be a hopeless wreck without Your Word and promises to fulfill my life with joy and peace. I love You because You first loved me. Help me through these next few months, and be with me through any pain and trials. Let me be a light to others and share Your love (Matthew 5:16).

Alone

Have you ever felt alone? Why do you sometimes feel alone even when you're with friends? Do you feel that they don't or won't understand—that no one understands? That's the moment. That's the moment to open the Bible and read. Read any verse you turn to because what you read will create an instant peace in your heart. The Lord is our Healer! Stop pushing Him away in self-pity. We say we put our hope in the Lord, yet we sulk and complain about being lonely.

Hebrews 10:23 says, "Let us hold unswervingly to the hope we profess, for he who promised is faithful."

The feeling of loneliness can be a trial for us and our faith. "God tries our faith so we can try his faithfulness" (Author unknown). Try God's faithfulness; it'll amaze you! God is here, and anything can happen.

As a Christian, we are held to a John 6:29 standard: "Jesus answered, 'The work of God is this: to believe in the one he has sent.'" Do it! Believe. It will calm your heart and bring you joy. We can be joyful knowing where we are going and who our Father is. Think of those who do not know. They don't have that joy!

Do not be lonely. The Lord is near—and even closer when you choose to open your heart to Him and listen, talk, and love.

> Lord, thank You for always being with me even when I feel so alone. Embrace me in Your arms, and allow me to be filled with Your love and comfort. You are for me, and I love You. Thank You for Your faithfulness, love, and mercy (Psalm 62:2).

When was a time that you began to feel lonely and experienced the Lord? It's important to remember when the Lord comes through during our "valley" moments, so we strengthen our faith and walk with Him. Use the space below to write about it.

Galatians 1:4

Jesus gave His life for our sins, just as God our Father planned, in order to rescue us from this evil world in which we live.

—Galatians 1:4

For as long as I can remember, I've been taught that Jesus died for our sins because He loves us and is saving us from eternal damnation. Yes, I believe it. No, I don't appreciate it like I should. What am I doing on those days when I'm mad at God for whatever stupid reason I have? What am I thinking when I doubt that He can save me from whatever I'm dealing with? Today I'm making a vow to focus on appreciating everything more. Not just what God has done for me, but others as well: people who let me go ahead of them in the grocery line, people who smile at me or ask about my day. If we appreciate the little things in life, we'll be ten times happier. I feel terrible that I slip from doing that all the time.

Now, I'm taking a few minutes in prayer and appreciation of Christ and His sacrifice. I can't wrap my mind fully around all of it, but I will thank Him and praise Him for this life and for His Son, who died for me. I can't help but weep when I think about it, and pure joy overwhelms my soul!

Lord, I'm sorry for my days where I don't appreciate Your love and provision. You alone deserve all of the glory and honor and praise. Please forgive my human brokenness, and thank You so much for never giving up on me. Your unconditional love for me in my brokenness is healing and all-powerful. I love You (Psalm 146:1).

Ask. Seek. Knock.

Ask and it will be given to you; seek and you will find;
knock and the door will be opened to you.
—Matthew 7:7

So often when I read this verse I only halfway understood. I mean I knew how to ask. I knew how to seek, but when it came to knocking, I wasn't so sure. Well, as I listened to my wonderful Francis Chan podcasts, I began to understand better.

1. I learned that I need to be persistent in asking for my needs to be according to God's will. You know how they say persistence is key? Well it is. Being persistent in prayer will keep you focused on prayer and more aware of when God answers it.
2. When seeking, I must put into action my request. Work for what I want, and if it is God's will, He will answer in His perfect time.
3. Knocking is continually asking along the way as you work for your prayer request. My cousin has cancer, and I refuse to believe the doctors when they give bad reports. I know God will and can pull through for her and bring glory to His name through healing.*

God will answer in His time and in His way. We must be persistent in prayer and live by faith, not by sight (as hard as that may be). It's okay to pray for the impossible. I also learned to be widow-like in my praying. That means that I don't depend on anyone else when it comes to my prayer life. I need to be completely trusting Christ and His provision. The gospel clearly states that we can be released from our old selves, which is extremely

7

encouraging to me. We may not be completely secure in our lives, but that's why security in Christ and prayer is so important.

> I love You, Father, even when I don't understand Your plan. It is perfect and anointed. Thank You for provision and love and healing. I will be strong because You are my Rock. Anoint me with comfort and grace and the confidence to pray for the impossible (1 Thessalonians 5:17).

THOUGHTS, THOUGHTS
& MORE THOUGHTS.

Have you ever heard the phrase "Take every thought captive to make it obedient to Christ" (2 Corinthians 10:5)? I have been reminded of this verse numerous times in the past week, from various people and in a variety of situations. Tonight I finally sat down and prayed about what God is trying to tell me through all these reoccurring events centered on this verse. A lot of new things are happening, and my life feels extremely overwhelming and confusing sometimes. If I went into detail my fingers would fall off, so I'll just leave it at that. When I ponder over what to do in each situation or relationship, my mind floods with different ways to handle things. I get frustrated and upset and I know God is crying out to me with comfort and the peace that passes all understanding, yet I wallow. The God of the UNIVERSE is telling me, "I will carry you, and I will sustain you by My power in the ways that I have chosen and prepared for you. YOU SHALL NOT TAKE EVEN THE FIRST STEP IN YOUR OWN STRENGTH" (taken from *Come Away My Beloved* by Francis J. Roberts). Satan is saying the complete opposite, forcing me to feel like I am on my own and have to make the right choice or say the right thing or I'm a failure. If you start feeling this way, STOP and open your Bible, pray— do SOMETHING to connect with the Father, because the longer you sit in Satan's presence, where your human nature doesn't stand a chance, the easier it becomes to slip into temptation and sin.

Matthew 16:23 tells of a time that Jesus was telling the disciples about the coming of His death, and Peter didn't want to hear it because it upset him. Jesus replied: "Get behind me Satan! You are a stumbling block to me; for you are setting your mind not on divine things but on human things."

I cringe at how often I set my mind not on divine things, but on human things. God does not put negative thoughts in your mind. When you question the Truth or His power, that isn't Him, but Satan. The moment that's most difficult to read Scripture is when you need self-discipline to discover the comfort and joy of the Living God.

BUT WAIT! Satan doesn't stop there. Sometimes whatever you were worried about takes your mind off of the focus of God and His Word and shifts it to what you originally were concerned about. CONTINUE IN THE WORD so that Satan isn't satisfied!

Malachi 4:2 says … the Sun of Righteousness will arise with healing in His wings.

Rejoice in the Lord and let your lips praise Him in song.

Taking your thoughts captive takes work and constant perseverance in the Word, but the more disciplined you are, the more the Truth radiates in your mind and in your heart. The wisdom of the Lord will soon become the first thing you seek when a problem or worry arises.

Lord, I rejoice in you and sing your praises with my lips. Thank you for being my Strength and Salvation always and forever. I'm always on your heart, and your praise is always on my tongue. Thank you for healing and love.

SLUMPS & SALVATION

I've been in a slump—a faith slump. If you've never been in one, I would be surprised. Lately, I've been pushing away my Bible and holding back on prayer, afraid of what God might tell me. I haven't boldly approached the throne because I've been fearful of what God might call me to do. And it's caused me sadness. I've been grieving lately because I don't want to be in a slump. I want to be alive and filled with energy, and I want everyone around me to see Jesus in my eyes. SO, I dragged myself to church tonight. It's there, in church, that I've been on an incredible roller coaster ride of finding myself through my faith and finding love for others and Lord Jesus.

In fact, it was there, at a conference, that Satan found the opportunity to attack in a big way. This conference was life-changing, eye-opening, and heart-wrenching. I grew so much in two days that I was in constant prayer and praise and shed tears of joy. Then, as I exited through the doors on the last day, Satan showed up bigger than ever, by putting so much self-doubt in my mind that I went into an instant faith slump. At church camp, kids always leave with a "Jesus high," and, sadly, it often slowly fades. This slump began as soon as I left one of the greatest weekends of my life. Before I left the conference, I had emailed the pastor about meeting with him regarding some lessons. I wanted affirmation that they were from Christ, not from my human desires. He agreed to meet with me, but by the time we emailed about a specific time to meet, the conference was over, and the slump had begun. I didn't want to talk anymore; I was feeling too *blah*. I'm not sure how to describe it, but I was miserable.

I left to visit my home in Louisiana for a month, and a million and twelve things happened, good and bad. I dragged myself to a worship service in an attempt to press toward the Lord harder than ever and command Satan to flee. I wanted to feel like myself again. The message was the exact thing that I needed (naturally, God does that).

It's okay to grieve or be sad if you're going through something. You don't need to sugar coat it when you're talking to God. You can be raw and honest and broken. Jesus used PIECES of bread to feed over 5,000. He doesn't need you to come to Him whole. You can come to Him in pieces. When you are upset or in distress about something, the world tells you to ease your grief with addiction or old habits, but grief can't be ignored. No amount of worldly comfort will ever be healing. Healing is all in God's hands. We need courage to face our problems, even with the Lord's strength, and it's a daily battle to give them to God. That's one of the hardest things in the universe to do. I often put off prayer, so God doesn't make me deal with the situation or put me in the middle of my pain. But He puts me there because when HE gives me power to prevail, I won't fear that situation or pain if it comes again. We often try to sanitize our grief, but it's okay to cry it out and get it all out, because life isn't always what we want it to be. I encourage you to grieve with hope. You are a child of the most high God. Even when it's the last thing you want to do, fight for your relationship with Him and fight for healing through Christ Jesus.

How long will you be in prison for your mistake?

Where the Spirit of the Lord is, there is liberty.

I can always trust that you will meet me where I am, Father. In heartbreak and sorrow to joy and laughter, you are there to hold me and tend to my heart. Thank you for being such a perfect healer and protector of your children. Your name is above all names, I love you.

2 Corinthians 3:1

ONE HOUR CAN CHANGE EVERYTHING

This morning I slept in instead of going to a new church I'd been attending for a few weeks. I love that church and the people, but I was feeling a little hopeless. I should've sucked it up and gone because I firmly believe it could've changed everything. I know what I would've heard would have been applicable. I know I would've loved it. But I didn't go, and the hour that I slept in changed everything. We all have days when we just can't get ourselves out of bed. I just want to encourage you to be stronger than I was—get up and go. God works in your weakness AND courage.

I wonder what would happen if I just spent one hour with a stranger. Asking them about who they are and how they became that person. Sharing my testimony and maybe, just maybe, (for both of us) it could change everything.

I woke up this morning feeling very awake and ready for the day—at 1pm. I haven't slept that late in a long time, so I felt like the day was gone. And for today, that changed everything.

I'm going to a church tonight with a new friend.

One hour that I should've been in church. One hour that I could talk to a stranger. One hour of rest. One hour of Truth.

ONE HOUR CAN CHANGE EVERYTHING.

How will you spend all the hours in one day? There are twenty-four— eight for sleeping. Whose life will you change? Will it be your own because of your strength and courage?

"Be the change you wish to see in the world." – Gandhi

2 Corinthians 5:17 "Therefore, if anyone is in Christ, the new creation has come: the old has gone, the new is here!"

I rejoice in the time you give us to do your work, Father. I pray for open eyes and ears for missions you have for me. I pray that I see miracles and witness supernatural change in people's lives as a testament to your active love. Strengthen my faith so I may pour out on others the joy you give me. Thank you Jesus!

Have you ever encountered someone who changed your life even through one conversation? What were they like? Would you want to adopt some attributes like theirs?

12 MOSQUITO BITES LATER

Shooting Stars. Lightening Bugs. Lake Water. Fireworks.

The dock wood is hard but not terribly uncomfortable. I lay there alone last night, watching the fireworks and just being by myself for the first time in a long time. The verse that came to mind is to be "still" and know that He is God (Psalm 46:10). Ever tried that? To be still? for MORE than five minutes? It's my personal agony. I don't mean just your body. I mean your mind, too. My mind can jump from one topic to another so fast I have to backtrack and figure out how it even got there! Ridiculous. And it's always the most random things! Anyway, I lay on the dock and stayed still. I got to talk to the Creator of it all—of the water under me, the trees to my right and the air that keeps me alive. Weird how it all works together. I got to thank Him. I never take enough time to do that. Do you? I know it's hard to "find time" to pray or get in the Word, but imagine if you only talked to your mom one day a week for five minutes or less, your entire life—not much of a relationship, huh?

Think about the word Creator. What if you created something and you were so proud that you wanted to show it off everywhere you went to everyone, but that object never thanked you for its creation or spoke to you at all. (not that I could create anything that spoke, but you know what I mean).

I encourage you to be still. Know that He is God. He is your Creator. He is your Father.

Thank you, Father. Thank you. Thank you for your perfect creation, the life you breathed in me, and for a moment to be still. Forgive me for not taking enough time to honor and glorify your name. I love you.

Psalm 46:10

GET IT

There's just something about witnessing a kid's life change for the glory of the Lord. Something about seeing eyes light up and a smile get a little brighter than before. The inward emotion of the heart glows through them and the conversations all of a sudden become richer. They start to "get it." There are so many things I don't get 100 percent but I'm still learning and the more I learn, the more in love with the Lord I fall. When a kid finally feels the love of the Lord above all earthly love and acceptance, a relief and a certain type of joy falls upon them. They realize that no matter who is around them or who may be cutting them down, the Creator of the universe thinks they are worth something, and let's face it, that's pretty cool. The part that saddens my heart is that some people never truly "get it." They go through life confused and maybe spiteful towards God because of the things in their life. Or maybe they think they "get it" and act like they do, but something in their heart doubts and isn't truly accepting of the Father's love. I'm not saying you're wrong if you doubt because sometimes that can sharpen your faith depending on the depth you go into to discover the Truth. I'm saying that they have hardened hearts toward God and don't even give believing a chance. I'm also not saying I know everything, by any means, but I do know who my Father is and where I will spend eternity. I pray you know the same, but I really want you to think about it ...

What life are you living?

Do you "get it"?

Or are you just playing the part and pretending to?

Embrace the love of the Lord and find security in His arms, rather than the earthly things consuming your time and efforts. All will disappoint except the Lord and His love and restoration.

Thank you, Jesus.

Thank you Jesus for accepting and loving your children even when we don't always reciprocate as passionately and excitedly as you always are when you love us. I pray for clarity and understanding of you and your perfect nature as I journey to discover more of you. Give me more of you, Father. Thank you for your love and sacrifice.

1 John 4:8

SIMON SAYS

Simon says, "Hop on one foot." Remember that game? Simple instructions and everyone who played obeyed. If you didn't, you were out. Couldn't play anymore.

What if Jesus kicked us out of Christianity if we didn't do what He said? Make disciples of men. Honor your father and mother. OR YOU'RE OUT. Can't be a Christian anymore.

Whoa.

I'm really thankful for His mercy. Thankful for His grace.

Why is it so difficult to do what Jesus said? Why do we feel like all we need to do with the Word of God is read and memorize? Maybe, if you're advanced, learn the Greek version of the word. WHY IS THIS AS SERIOUS AS WE TAKE IT?? The Word of God is a call to action! It's not a suggestion, it's truth. Jesus COMMANDS.

Why do we doubt it's truth when we suffer? When we are walking in the power of Christ, we expect it to be roses and daises, and as soon as it gets hard we want to quit. Is life not harder without Christ? Mine seems to be. 1 Peter 4:12-19 is on my heart today because for the past few months I've had to fight with everything I have to stay disciplined in the Word. I saw so many kids get saved this summer, but a part of me still felt distant from the Lord. It was HARD to get in the Word. It was HARD to pray. But today I finally broke down and wept as I listened to Francis Chan preach on 1 Peter because who am I to expect not to have to work on my faith? Why do I think happiness will be handed to me? Growing in your faith takes work and determination. It's more rewarding than anything, but you may not see it while you're in the middle of a storm. Expect hardship and be thankful for the title "Christian" and be thankful that if you mess up or do something wrong, God isn't going to kick you out of the faith; rather He will embrace you and say, "I forgive you, let's continue on our walk together."

Dear friends, do not be surprised at the fiery ordeal that has come on you to test you, as though something strange were happening to you. But rejoice inasmuch as you participate in the sufferings of Christ, so that you may be overjoyed when his glory is revealed. If you are insulted because of the name of Christ, you are blessed, for the Spirit of glory and of God rests on you. If you suffer, it should not be as a murderer or thief or any other kind of criminal, or even as a meddler. However, if you suffer as a Christian, do not be ashamed, but praise God that you bear that name. For it is time for judgment to begin with God's household; and if it begins with us, what will the outcome be for those who do not obey the gospel of God? And, if it is hard for the righteous to be saved, what will become of the ungodly and the sinner?" So then, those who suffer according to God's will should commit themselves to their faithful Creator and continue to do good. I Peter 4:12-19

Now go. Do what JESUS says.

Forgive me, Lord, for not pursuing you wholeheartedly with passion and fire. Anoint me with a steadfast and consistent love and desire to be obedient and close to your heart. I know that you are for me and I pray that I learn to love and appreciate you so much more. Thank you for unconditional love and nearness.

"WE WERE LOST & I WAS FRUSTRATED"

(names changed)

Today I learned an amazing story that's too long to type but may have changed my life.

For a group project, I had to interview a homeless family. With my group, I had been volunteering there all semester. Families had been in and out so I met one family for the first time during the interview.

They were NOT always homeless. A year ago at this time, the father was buying their youngest daughter a scooter for Christmas. A nice scooter, not a razor like we had in middle school.

To make a long story short, they moved for the father to get a better job. The people who offered a place for them to stay changed their mind once they got to Nashville, leaving them homeless. The sweet Mother and their daughter went to the women's shelter, and the father went to the men's. They were separated and confused as to how they got to this place. They couldn't see each other much, and it was a hard thing for each one of them. Their five-year old daughter was getting beat up in the shelter, and they had never dreamed of being in such a situation. Every night she prayed, "Lord, just let me get my baby out of here."

"Never take anything for granted," they said. "You realize how blessed you are when it's all gone. I slept in the car most nights, but I'd look around and be thankful, because some guys didn't even have a car to sleep in."

The father and I bonded over dreads (if you know me, you know I love dreads), and I learned so much from him about his love for his family and Jesus. He talked about prayer and blessings and just really opened my eyes to what's around me.

I'm so thankful for shelter and the things I have surrounding me. I pray I never take this for granted, though walking into my apartment made me sick and sitting here on a computer is making me feel terrible.

This is just a tiny bit of our conversation and barely scratches the surface. They gave us the G rated version of the story and told us about some things that broke his heart about the situation, and I had to stop myself from crying about fifteen times. Being professional isn't that easy in those types of interviews.

Please join me in praying for sweet families that have lost everything. I'm humbled by their joy and laugher, and thankful I got to meet them.

Lord, I specifically pray over the Smith family and their journey. I pray over their hearts and financial stability. I pray over any of your children who need financial security, and I pray blessing over their bank accounts. Thank you for always providing and also for giving us a glimpse into the world we live in and the effort we can make to improve its state. Thank you in advance for blessings Father, thank you for being so wonderful and all-powerful!!

Luke 12:24

PUPPIES & GRACE

Romans 5:20 (The Message) " ...But sin didn't, and doesn't have a chance in competition with the aggressive forgiveness we call grace. When it's sin versus grace, grace wins hands down."

Time out. I've reread " ...the aggressive forgiveness we call grace ..." over and over and I'm floored every time. I've never thought about describing grace like that. It's like this: I think of grace as a cuddly warm blanket that God wraps us in because we are the shivering cold dog shaking from being wet and outside in the snow. (dibs on being the Shiba Inu Pup)

But when I think about calling it "aggressive forgiveness," I imagine how passionate God is for us, and He is just arms wide open yelling, "I LOVE YOU! I FORGIVE YOU! THERE'S NOTHING THAT CAN SEPARATE YOU FROM MY LOVE!!!" and I get all goosebumpy. Then I picture Him fighting for us against the enemy and claiming us as His children. That aggressive forgiveness just blows my mind!

The dictionary defines grace as simple elegance or something like that. PSHHH! God's grace is full of love and passion and desire to allow us to walk with Him and accept His grace and, in turn, pour it out to others. Instead of giving out warm grace blankets to cold puppies, maybe we should show passionate grace, full of love and excitement. I'm not exactly sure what that looks like just yet, but I guess it's different for everyone. For me, that means repairing old relationships and loving the unlovable.

What does it look like for you to show aggressive forgiveness aka GRACE?

Thank you, Father, for your never ending grace and love. I'm so unworthy, but so honored and thankful for crazy, amazing, unaltered grace!!!

Jeremiah 31:2-3

DON'T LISTEN TO YOUR HEART

Jeremiah 17:9 The heart is deceitful above all things and beyond cure. Who can understand it?

This is tough. I've always been taught to "listen to your heart," but when I logically think about it, this verse is so true. My head says no and my heart says yes, and nine times out of ten my logic is what I should've gone with. I hate when I get excited over a text or a call from someone I know isn't a good influence or when I see younger girls do the same. I wish I could put my heart on mute or something.

Here's where I get excited though. The Lord is so so powerful, that He can fill whatever void I'm trying to fill. HE CAN BREAK ALL CHAINS. I feel so loved when I think about the freedom offered with Christ. Now all I have to do is embrace it and teach my heart some logic!

Thank you for guidance and love when my human nature is tempted by one thing and you say another. Thank you for filling voids and creating a space for your love and fulfillment in my heart and life! I pray for my friends, family, and everyone around me to break chains in their lives and surrender to your love and grace!

ROMANS 8

Literally, in the past three sermons I have heard, Romans 8 was mentioned. When the Lord is trying to speak to you, He don't play. Anyway, I sat down and thought, "Hmm ... what should I read for devo this morning? DUH! ROMANS 8!" So I opened to it and began. I intended to stop at verse 11, but continued to read until the end of 17. The verses that hit me the most were Romans 8:1,5, 6, 17.

Verse 17 has one word in the NIV version and ESV version that stood out to me.

"and if children, then heirs- heirs of God and fellow heirs with Christ, provided we SUFFER with Him in order that we may also be glorified with Him."

Suffer.

So, I know I've heard this verse so many times, but so often I get back into the mindset of "I shouldn't be sad or lonely or upset because I'm a Christian and I should always be happy knowing I'm a child of God." YES, I am a child of God, but this doesn't mean I'm going to be happy 100 percent of the time. If a Christian is *Hakuna Matata* all the time, something is wrong. As Christians, we are in a battle! A battle of spiritual warfare and THAT IS TOUGH! That requires strength and determination. We are under constant attack! My main sufferings come from my own struggle, my friends' and family's struggles, knowing there are people in this world who are lost, knowing there are people in my immediate family and friends that are lost, etc. It hurts my heart to see other people struggle, and I should be praying fervently for them! Praying without ceasing! Did I forget what that is? 24/7, all the time! Does that sound extreme? So does my Savior DYING for me.

We can't expect complete happiness and bliss, but we can expect heavenly joy and peace through chaos and an ever present need and desire to lean on the Lord so that He will be glorified through our suffering.

Lord, when I suffer I sometimes forget how close you are. I forget you're with me in the storm, and I pray against the temptation and habit of doing that. Thank you for fighting with and for me. I pray for constant communication and passion for you!

COMMUNITY GROUPIN'

I miss the attitude I had when I first moved to Nashville. I was going to new places by myself and exploring with such wonder and hope. It was fun for a while, but the hope soon turned to doubt and the wonder turned to boredom, because as great as these places were, I didn't have anyone to share them with.

I fear that's what happens to so many people's faith. They experience the Lord and all of His life-changing holiness, and there isn't anyone around them that feels the same way or understands the power of saving grace. After a few weeks in Nashville, I wanted to share my new experiences and growth with someone, but I didn't know anyone. At first, it was just me and the Lord and it was so fruitful and exciting, but when no one was there to keep me accountable or listen to my joy and affirm it, I didn't get to talk about it often. While the light didn't die by any means, it was dimmed by my surroundings and people discouraging spiritual growth. Although I didn't agree with them, I fell subject to the spiral of silence.

Then I began walking with a church family. I'm SO thankful for them and the community I've gotten to be a part of. I go to a community group where we encourage and pray for one another. We listen and we respond with God-filled answers and it's like my cup is being replenished every week. Don't get me wrong, I do not think that the Lord could not do this on His own. I just know that it's His will that I have a community of believers around me and that's what He gave me. I'm still praying for people who are like close friends I left behind, my Bridgets and Gennifers, to show up, but for now, I will soak in thankfulness for Community groups.

All this to say, it's very important to be in a community of believers. I don't mean people who say they are, I mean people who will lay hands on you and pray aloud with you and ask you how you are and how everything is going and seriously care. It makes ALL the difference, trust me!

When I was in a dark place, I confessed this to my group and they were with me and they cared and asked and blessed me! When the Lord broke those chains, they were the ones I couldn't wait to tell and they affirmed my strength and rejoiced with me. Isn't it obvious the importance of having a group to share things with? If you're going to go out in this world and spread the Gospel, it's likely that you will be persecuted and attacked. It's necessary to have people who back you up and love on you, taking you back to the hope and re-opening the sense of wonder that was found at the beginning of your walk.

Thank you for community, Jesus, for people who will cry and laugh and love together. I pray each and every person finds a community in your love and provision. Thank you, Father!

Romans 12:4-5

Who is in your community of encouragers and Godly friendships?

BLINKING LINES & A DIRTY SPONGE

I sat staring at that blinking line on the computer screen, the one that marks the place on the page before you begin typing, for probably five minutes. It was waiting for something, but what? Pure brilliance to fill up my mind to the point of overflow so my fingers had no choice but to write it down? Or maybe it was waiting for something, anything really. Attention. It was just so bored with sitting, blinking, that it wanted some sort of work or task to achieve. I've been that line before. I actually feel most like that line now, wanting any task or person to work for and absorb attention from. Why isn't the overwhelming love and compassion of the Lord enough for my human desires? I mean it is, but why can't my brain comprehend that? Sometimes I get so mad at myself for allowing things to come in front of my relationship with the Lord. I beat myself up thinking, "HE IS ENOUGH. STOP WANTING ANYTHING ELSE EVER AT ALL EXCEPT FOR THE LORD'S LOVE AND AFFECTION!" He is enough. That is true, but it's natural for me to want something on this earth. A good job or a husband or at LEAST a boyfriend, yeah? I often forget, during this self-destructive beating, that these are the times that are the steps to the pinnacle of awe. When I doubt, when I wonder or question, when I think about what I don't have, the Lord uses these times so that when He reveals Himself and His plan, it slaps me across the face and I have no choice or other desire than to worship, and He squeezes those doubts out like a wet sponge and refills me with pure and sweet brokenness for this world and frees me from my human nature. This seems temporary because a week later I'm back to being the gross sponge that stinks up the whole kitchen, but the most awe striking thing is that the Lord never gives up and continues to wring me out and start over with me, keeping the awe alive. So as I sit in my human rebellion, wondering and waiting for my awe moment, I'll be steadfast in my quiet time, and fight for my relationship with the Lord. It's not easy and sometimes (if I'm honest) it's the last thing I want to do, but when I buckle down and just do it, I always feel blessed. It never fails. I do wish I would never let something get in front of the Lord in my life, but I appreciate the Lord not giving up on me and stirring my heart to experience awe moments.

You are enough, Father. Thank you for the reminder, and thank you for being more than enough and loving me and telling me that I am more than enough as well.

1 Peter 3:8

WORD

If there's one thing I have a passion for, it's words. Accompanied by melodies, sure, but even without the music, words are art. They can do SO many things. The Lord SPOKE the earth into existence and healed sick and lame invalids. Does that not amaze anyone? He told stories with words and changed lives. The written Word of God is ALIVE. His WORD is TRUTH.

Words hold so much weight. I sometimes feel like I value words more than oxygen because when you die, oxygen can't continue in your lungs, but words can follow you forever. Your words are your legacy. What you said, wrote, sang, etc. Words can be tossed around or carefully planned, to heal or to hurt. They cause pain and joy. Everyone wants to know what a baby's first word was. What someone's last word was. Someone's words can instantly change a mood, create a smile, ruin a day.

So, what do you have to say?

Thank you Lord that with words you spoke creation into being and wrote the Bible. I pray that as I walk through life, I use my words for encouraging others, enabling the spiritual gifts you've bestowed upon me, and making sure that I am building up other people and glorifying your name.

Proverbs 18:21

NO GRUDGE TO HOLD

"it's not my grudge to hold"

This phrase struck me by surprise this morning. I mean I'm already really bad at holding grudges because I forget what happened in the first place, but I know many people are grudge-holding pro's. If we, as Christians, are called to forgive, then grudges shouldn't even be in our realm of attitude or desire. AND if anyone were allowed to hold a grudge, shouldn't it be Jesus who we basically slap in the face on a daily basis—and He DIED for us? So that girl that talked behind your back seems a lot less dramatic right? Maybe we have been treated poorly, but so was Jesus and He forgave so if we want to forgive and be forgiven, we can't be holding grudges!!

Just my thought for today.

(though it's taking all I have not to hold a grudge against my tire that rudely popped on my way home last night -_-)

Lord, allow my heart to receive and give forgiveness as a pouring out of your love to others. I pray that my walk is an example of your grace and power and pray that other people see YOU in my life. Thank you for not holding grudges!

Proverbs 16:24

WRESTLING—& LOSING

TRUSTING THE LORD IS HARD!

There, I said it. Me and God are in a wrestling match, and I'm losing pretty quickly. But honestly, one of my favorite places to be is wrestling with God because you can't wrestle with someone that's far away. He is near and He is powerful. I wish I could find joy in his presence right now, but I just want to cry in it and cry uncle and just collapse in His arms like a noodle.

If you've ever wrestled with God, don't think that's a bad thing. Be comforted in knowing that He's with you, and He will give you the grace to get through what He's confronted you with. I'm ready to learn the lesson and skip the hard stuff, but He doesn't work that way.

Thank you, Lord, for loving me enough to be near and wrestle with me in my darkest hours. Your greatness is unfathomable, and I'm so thankful to be able to communicate with you freely and honestly. Stay near me, Father, because I am yours and need you now more than ever.

Colossians 3:15

Have you ever been in a wrestling match with God? What was it like?

CONFESSION

I have to confess something. I still struggle with the same sin and temptations as I did two years ago, three years ago, five years ago. I think as Christians we kick ourselves for struggling over the same thing, and we get so discouraged in our walk, but I just want everyone to know that that isn't uncommon. You're okay and you're still forgiven even though you haven't conquered the sin that so easily entangles you. You're still loved. You're still beautiful. You're still worthy. DO NOT believe the devil's lies that tell you that you're unforgivable. REBUKE that. You are forgiven. The cross was more than enough, so don't think for a second that it wasn't enough to cover that sin.

Matthew 9:22: Jesus turned and saw her. "Take heart, daughter," he said, "your faith has healed you." And the woman was healed at that moment.

Our faith has healed us, y'all. Just keep running back to Jesus and you will overcome.

Thank you, Father, for healing and comfort! I'll continue to press forward with you, hand in hand, to stay strong and remain faithful to your will.

MAYBEIT'SJUSTMEBUT MAYBEIT'SYOUTOO

Sometimes I do this really dumb thing in life where everything is going exactly how I dreamed and my heart is full and I'm so content that I ignore God (just in case He plans on taking it away for some reason, I want Him to know that I probably would hate that), and then this life that I've always dreamed of and this contentment slowly turns into maximized insecurities, anxiety, and weird mood swings that send me into a roller coaster of myself outside of these "perfect" circumstances. Then, I surrender and go read a devotional and the Lord just calls me back and forgives me and loves on me and all of a sudden, the insecurities turn to confidence and the anxiety turns to happiness and the mood swings turn into joy and I realize how dumb I am for ignoring the Lord in the first place because I know who my Healer is and I know who my God is, but sometimes it's just so hard to feel like you need Him when life is going so perfectly. But the reality is, when we think we have it under control, the Lord usually shows us just how out of control we are, forcing us to fall back on Him, which is where we should've been in the first place. I'm so thankful for a God that reminds me of His constant love and compassion for His children, despite their rebellion. So so thankful and honored to be a child of the Most High.

I'm humbled by your love and grace and patience, Father. I praise your name and all that you've given your children!! Forgive my inconsistencies and fill my heart with faith and compassion!

1 John 4:18

A FEW THINGS

Despite the insanity that is life right now with high highs and low lows, I've felt the insane power and love of Christ. Through prayer, friends, family, guidance, and a supernatural peace, He has shown Himself so much. I'm so guilty of expecting Him to take away pain as soon as I pray or lean on Him. I just want it gone and I expect Him to just remove it immediately, but that's not how it works. He isn't there like a magic eraser, He's there to walk beside you THROUGH it. I think of it as a physical wound. If you don't want a scar, you rub ointment everyday/multiple times a day or whatever, but the first time you put that ointment on it, the scar doesn't immediately disappear. It's a process, and it takes discipline to keep reapplying, and it takes patience to know that it will eventually heal, but it will take time.

Just the same, asking God to heal you isn't an immediate resolution; it's a process and will take time.

The future is a scary thing for me right now, but the encouragement of my family and friends has helped and reminded me that the Lord is walking beside me if I just notice Him and take His hand. Easier said than done? That's what I thought, until I reached out and did it. There are still some panic moments, but not as many as I know I'd experience without the Lord's hand. It's so crazy how awesome He is.

Thank you for processes and storms and journeys, Lord! Thank you for growth and lessons and wisdom! I don't always understand and I'm not always thankful, but I'm working towards dancing in your Reign!

Lamentations 3:31-32

THANKFUL

. . . .

I'm so thankful that God loves me despite my inconsistent pursuit of Him. I'm so thankful it's not an earthly, passing love, but a love so deep that not a single thing can shift it. Does that blow anyone else's mind? I've let so many people down and so many have done the same to me and friendships have come and gone, but the only true consistent thing in my life is the Lord's love for me. He's so incredibly good to us though we ignore Him or disobey or what have you. I try so hard to understand why and I just don't. I'm not meant to. We are so undeserving, and He just fills up my heart to the brim. I'm not saying I don't struggle or let emotions lead sometimes. I do, but my awe comes in when He loves me through all of that. So incredible.

Thank you Jesus!

What are you thankful for? Use the space below to write about things you're thankful for:

LOVE/FEAR

1 John 4:18: There is no fear in love. But perfect love drives out fear, because fear has to do with punishment.

I was reading 1 John 4:18 tonight and I think roughly 1,000,000,000,000,000 different thoughts ran through my head about this verse. There is not fear in love but perfect love casts out fear. Immediately I want to think earthly love and the effects of fear on the various areas of that, but I have to back track and remember God is love and if I replace love with the word God in that verse, it takes on this heavenly meaning that is so much bigger, brighter, and bolder than any earthly love I ever imagine! Remembering God as (perfect) love is the absence of fear and the one thing I'm rebuking left and right lately is fear. Jesus, I refuse to operate in fear in any area because YOU hold my heart, life, and future. I believe that YOU cast out fear and your love is so perfect and holy that fear cannot stand in your presence. I want to be so consumed with your love that fear is a foreign concept. Switching my mind from earthly to heavenly when thinking about this verse physically lifted some fear off of my heart which may sound strange, but I promise I'm not exaggerating. My mindset completely shifted, as it does when thinking that way, but I encourage us all to remember the heavenly aspect of this love instead of our earthly love that is so so small in comparison.

JEREMIAH 29:11-12

"For I know the plans I have for you," declares the LORD, "plans to prosper you and not to harm you, plans to give you hope and a future. Then you will call on me and come and pray to me, and I will listen to you."

If you've heard any Bible verses at all, you've probably heard Jeremiah 29:11-12. Are you quoting it in your head right now? Thought so. Actually, it's sometimes just Jer. 29:11 but this morning I was reading my "Praying for Your Future Husband" book and it asked what stood out about Jeremiah 29:11-12. This verse that I've read and heard over and over and over and over. I mean people quote it after every stage of life, during seasons of doubt, seasons of change, etc. And after passing middle school, graduating high school, moving to a different state AND finishing college, I've heard it a lot. Anyway, I almost didn't even open the Bible to reread it because I have it memorized but I was like, "Eh, I should just open the Book," so I did and this one word jumped right off the page and slapped me in the face. "THEN" small word, big meaning. It's the first word in verse 12 and it comes AFTER God tells us that He has plans for us. So He says that He knows the plans He has for us. They are not a mystery floating about in heaven waiting for Him to just pick up and figure out. HE KNOWS THEM. AND they are GOOD! Imagine that, our God wanting GOOD for us, His children. His plans aren't to harm us, but are to give us hope and a future. So that's all great, then the small but big word. THEN, we will call on Him and come and pray to Him and He will listen. SO, I'm just catching myself here because I know He has plans for me and I ask Him all the time for this and that (whatever desires of my heart happen to be at the moment) and I don't just stop and think that my calling on Him and praying comes AFTER His plans. He says in the verse that His plan is already in place and He knows them. They aren't just a stranger on the street; He knows them and knows them well. Why am I over here saying, "Lord can you just give me the desire of my heart?" when I should be like, "Lord, let me fulfill this plan of yours because it is for my good and you already have this path laid out before me and if I just follow it, I will have hope and a future!" Why am I constantly saying, "Give me what I want" instead of, "Allow me to be obedient and receive what you have for me?" This honestly may not hit anyone as hard as it hit me this morning, but in a moment where I THINK I know what I want and when/how I want it, it was a great reminder to give it all to the Lord and HE will take care of His plan. All I have to do is obey.

Thank you for your plan and purpose for my life, Lord! Thank you for guidance and provision. I pray for the strength and perseverance to walk in your will!

MY CHAINS ARE GONE,
I'VE BEEN SET FREE!

Roughly eight journal pages and brain spills led me here. This weekend was filled with adventure, Jesus, self-discovery, and a lot of heart. I wish I remembered every detail, every word, every lesson but the main one I'm focusing on today is being free from the chains in my life. I finally identified that I've lived with chains of fear of abandonment on me for so long that it was like a light turned on in a dark, cobweb-filled attic full of old pictures and books. Lisa Harper was a guest speaker at Crosspoint Church this Sunday and my heart was so full after hearing her speak. I had a divine visit with a new friend Saturday, and we identified the fear of abandonment. Then Sunday Lisa spoke on breaking the chains in your life. How fitting and how gracious of Jesus to make it so clear to me that that's what I needed!! I prayed for the breaking of those chains and a renewed, bold heart for Jesus and naturally, like most things when you finally hit a breakthrough with them, the devil wants to attack. So I began to feel anxious this morning and I started praying and yes, this totally helped, but what always helps when you feel sick? Medicine. What's God's medicine? His Word!! So I started reading the Word and it was so healing and so happy! The devil is still trying to attack, but the more I fight for freedom through prayer and the Word, the more the conqueror will rise. Thank you Jesus for your grace and for great conversations with wonderful, God-filled people this weekend!

Thank you Jesus for your grace and for great conversations with wonderful, God-filled people!

Psalm 84:11

RAMBLING

The past 48ish hours have been insane in my world. Some of the most intense spiritual attacks I've ever felt. It was miserable. I have lived with my nose so deeply in the Bible I'm surprised the words aren't permanently stamped on my face, and I've been in so much prayer I've run out of things to say. I don't want this to sound like I feel so Holy because I don't. I was face down in my pillow crying so hard I could barely breathe and I didn't have any appetite at all— it was miserable. From Saturday until last night I heard the phrase "chain breaker" or "breaking chains" roughly ten times. The Lord wasn't just using the still small voice, but the varsity cheerleader megaphone to get my attention. Sitting in church last night I felt the Holy Spirit put His arm around me and just speak Truth in my life and remind me how close He is to me and my heart. I physically felt His arm, and it was so great. I didn't have a rush of emotions or tingles like sometimes happens, it was just comfort and a peace. I could relax and just hang out with my best friend. That kind of feeling. It was healing, and it was joyful. It was breaking chains of fear and of worry and allowing confidence that my heart desires are heard— and I respond "yes and amen!" If you're ever in Nashville on a Tuesday night, the Belonging is a place that's more than a church. It's an encounter with Jesus. This is basically what the sermon was on so that's fitting, but the main point is that the encounter can be anywhere, not just the Belonging. In your car, bedroom, church, or wherever!

Thank you Jesus for drawing me closer, breaking chains, and showing me how much you love me!! He's so at work with me and the people around me, it's so amazing!! Praiseeeee!

Matthew 6:31-32

IN THE WILDERNESS

I wish I could sit here and answer any and all questions with definitive, clear responses that help guide and direct you. Ha, I wish I could ask someone for the same things. Yes, I do believe that Jesus guides and directs my every step and holds my right hand as I walk, but I'm not going to say that's easy. I won't fluff it up and say, "Just listen to Jesus, and it'll all be okay." Well, that is the very exact truth, but again, it's not easy. I imagine Jesus and me walking hand in hand on a trail of some sort (I like hiking so let's go with that). He holds my right hand and I look up at him with bright eyes and the biggest smile as we are walking. I can't even look ahead to see where I'm going because I'm allowing Him to guide me. That's the ideal way to live life in my imagination. Even knowing what joy that brings me and even knowing that my happiest and most exciting days are the ones I spend the most time with Jesus, I sometimes glance away as we walk. Sometimes I bend down, pick up what I think is a jewel but it turns out to be mud. Sometimes I'm trying to fight through the brush with my left hand to try and see what's ahead. My control freak nature kicks in and all I want is answers. Clear, definitive answers. I'll be the first to admit that listening to the voice of God is not always easy. HOWEVER, I'll be the first to admit that hearing from Him is so fulfilling and brings so much freedom. During the looking away times and control freak times, He just looks at me, whispers, "trust me" and holds my hand even tighter. He doesn't let go. I remember moments where I heard direction so clearly and remembering that as I walk is going to be the key in continuing on the trail. I won't look behind except to remember the miracles and have the "remember when you told me this …?" laughing memories with Jesus. With humility and thankfulness, I'll look down at His hand and see where the sacrifice scarred Him, and I'll remember that hand has fashioned my future and present and it's so powerful and full of love that no matter what, I just need to listen to Jesus and it'll all be okay. Big decisions are ahead, Jesus. Let's walk.

I'm so thankful that you never let go, Father! I love adventuring with you and I pray for more amazing adventures!

Matthew 21:22

RUNNING WITH JESUS

Today my adventure with Jesus is just smiles. We are running. He knows I hate running so he straps on his Nikes and walks when I wanna walk and runs when I catch my breath. He's making me laugh by having butterflies fly around me every now and then. He's not even tripping on his robe!? What a superhero. He points out a blackberry bush and reminds me how faithful he is to provide for me. We're laughing at my lack of breath and how I forgot to eat a banana so I keep having dumb cramps. I'm not kidding when I tell you I hate running. He loves me still. I'm so happy to have my joy back. Life isn't perfect, and I don't have a perfect life. But joy transcends all of that and HIS joy fulfills, and it makes you smile for no reason and get a rush of happiness and love for everyone you see. I've made two friends so far (meaning had a conversation), a lady who made sure she didn't hit me which was nice, and an older gentleman just getting some shade and doing some yard work. Jesus waved too, "thank you daughter." "Good morning, son." They're his too. Remember that everyone you see, they're the Lord's creation and children. He loves them even if they don't love him. I don't remember that enough. Okay I've been walking the whole time I've been typing this so I should get back to at least a jog.

Onto mile 3.

Thank you for reminding me that you're absolutely everywhere with me and loving me through my craziness.

1 Corinthians 2:9

I STILL DON'T LIKE CHICK FLICKS
BUT SOMETIMES I'M WEAK

Tonight Jesus curled up on the couch with me to watch a movie. A movie I swore on my life I would never watch because I hate chick flicks and it's the new *The Notebook* for sure, but after a long day with a lot of emotions and confusion, He brought the hummus and I brought the tears. He said it was okay every now and then to just lose it. It's quite comforting when He reminds me that I don't have to be perfect and happy 24/7. We cried together, He held my hand and passed the tissues. He knows I lose myself in movies so easily so He didn't try to talk too much, but he also had to hug me a couple times when it got super sad. He reminded me through this movie how precious the people around me are. My family, friends, the handsome fella I get to hold hands with when we're in the same city, etc. He reminded me how He's at work in their lives and in the lives of the everyday people I see on the street or in this case, the beach. Los Angeles has been a three week period of lessons, memories, laughs, and tears. Hopes rode a roller coaster and dreams were still driving and arguing whether to turn left or right, singing JESUS TAKE THE WHEEEEEEEEL because I'm powerless. I'm not in control and I've got to get that through my skull. Sorry for being so stubborn, Abba. He's so great. I like our adventures, but I also like the valley walks together. The fun joyful stuff is great, but it's when He wipes away my tears that my heart feels so extremely held and cared for. My adventure with Jesus tonight was sweet and simple. Okay? ok.

I love you, Jesus, through the mountain tops and through the valleys. Thank you for loving me the same. I pray that I am an example of love to everyone around me!

Revelation 21:4

What's your latest adventure with Jesus?
(Use the space below to express your latest brain spills)

MISSIN YA

Tonight during worship Jesus gave me a little giggle and pat on the back. He was teaching me so much during worship and I kept wanting it to end so I could sit down and write it all down, and He just kept saying, "but I've been missin ya! I want to keep hearing you and holding your hand as you praise me!" And I'm all, "glory to the Father, can I sit so I can write down what you're teachin' me now Dad?!" And he's like, "just enjoy the moment and talk to me, daughter." And the desire ceases and I'm just singing to Him, spending time with him. Time I forgot I had access to. Intimate moments that I let guilt shame me from. That is not of the Lord!! Guilt and shame are solely lies planted by Satan and let me tell you what! Satan knows I'm a lie fighter so that's his favorite thing to throw at me. Well I'm going to one two punch those away and give my Jesus a big ole lap hug!

Thank you Jesus thank you Jesus!!!
Matthew 25:21

YOU & OTHERS

A LESSON FROM CONNER

I was on my way to write music. It was night. I needed gas and I didn't want to go alone to the gas station. My friend, Conner, lived close by, and he said he would go with me. While we were there, a man walked up to Conner with an empty red gas can and asked if he would help him out by putting some gas in it. Conner did. Not a minute after the first man walked away, a second man approached Conner asking for a sandwich. He got him one. Con proceeded to pump my gas, and then we were on our way. I felt that I needed to apologize, because I had taken him away from studying to come get gas, and then two men asked him to make a sacrifice. I didn't know how he felt about the situation, but his response was quite pleasing to me and, I would think, to the Lord, as well. Conner told me not to be sorry and that he was happy to help them and felt so humbled and blessed that he was given that opportunity for God to use him in that way. My mouth almost dropped to the floor, but I kept my composure. He continued to say how he felt like the second guy may have had a rough past. He was not there to judge him, only to give a hungry man food. Now, not only am I shocked, amazed, and thrilled that he is saying all this, but I'm feeling the Lord's love and presence. Conner showed Christ's love in a major way.

My grandfather has always been a man to show Christ's love in such ways, so to see a friend of mine do the same was inspiring. I usually give to the hungry or homeless as much as I can, but I was a mere witness to this and felt more blessed than I ever have when I gave to the needy. We are all needy in God's eyes. We need Him. We constantly cry out to Him in distress wanting mercy and love. Tonight these men asked Conner to provide for their needs as we ask God to provide for our needs. Imagine if

Conner had a bad attitude about it. Imagine if he had said no. Imagine if God would say no or blow us off.

Thank you, Father, for always providing for me and being there for me through any time of need. You are my Everything, and my Provider that never fails me! Thank you for Conner's friendship and giving heart. Thank you for showing your love through him tonight and blessing everyone that was there tonight at the gas station. YOU NEVER CEASE TO AMAZE ME, FATHER!!!

Philippians 4:9

DATING

So, there's this thing. It's popular in teen years and on into adulthood until eventually it lands you with one person for life. Most call this "DATING."

I have mixed emotions about the topic. Whether you should or shouldn't, when or when not to. Generally I would discourage dating as long as possible, because the more you give your heart away, the less you will have to give to the man or woman God has paired you with for life. You may ask "How will I meet him or her if I don't date?" I'm not saying don't date at all, I'm just saying God will put the man or woman in your life that you are meant to be with. Let Him do it and don't look for love yourself. God will create a better story for you if you let Him be the author. So often I've tried to take the pen away rather than rely on Him. Still do, really.

Phil. 1:9-10 says : And this is my prayer: that your love may abound more and more in knowledge and depth of insight, so that you may be able to discern what is best and may be pure and blameless until the day of Christ.

Which leads me into describing two types of dating or love—the first being "Smart love" and the other being "Dumb love."

Smart love is when you use your head and heart to pursue someone, recognizing when it's time to break up even if you don't want to, or knowing what you deserve and knowing your standards and NOT BREAKING THEM!

Dumb love is when you use your emotions to drive your relationship and don't think about what you're doing. Ultimately, your emotions may make you compromise your morals or stay in a relationship when you know you shouldn't.

It takes strength to initiate smart love. If your heart isn't strengthened by the Lord and His Word, then you are most likely not going to be a blessing to the other party. Don't you want to bless your boyfriend or girlfriend if you are going to engage in a relationship? If you aren't yet practicing smart love, I advise taking time to just be friends with the opposite sex until you are secure in your love with Christ. He will prepare your heart. I know waiting is not easy, but what in life is?

Now say you've made it to the point where you are able to practice smart love and you are on your second or third date and you share your first kiss. You may feel instantly in love, but are you? HERE IS WHERE YOU USE SMART LOVE! Think about it. Pray about it. DON'T RUSH!

I talked about being a blessing to the other person, but what about your needs? Hear me out: When we make God's glory and the needs of others a priority, we position ourselves to receive God's best in our lives as well.

In closing I say to trust God's timing in finding your soul mate. Focus on giving Glory to God rather than finding a boyfriend or girlfriend. God's got you.

Father, thank you for creating in me a heart made for love and honor. I thank you for your protection and relationship as I navigate through this crazy world. Please anoint me with wisdom and discernment for the hearts and people in my life. Allow me to care for them with grace and dignity. Thank you for the blessings you have bestowed upon me.

1 John 4:19

DAD vs GOD

In childhood, middle school, high school, and college, I have always had a level of respect for my grandfather and dad. I feel like everyone does. No one wants to disappoint their dad. I know I didn't. I wanted him to be proud of me. When I was in trouble, I would immediately start crying when my poppa would walk in to discipline me. I had a respectful fear of him. I never forgot to say "Yes, sir." When I was being disciplined or got in trouble and had to ask for forgiveness, I'd think about my actions and words carefully and how I would respond. I'd humble myself and be apologetic for my disobedience. I felt *unworthy*.

I was praying the other day and I was like, "Hey, God, please forgive me for my sins and thanks for all you do for me and I love you! kthanksbye." Then I was listening to a Francis Chan podcast when it hit me like a train. WHY ON EARTH WAS I MORE RESPECTFUL AND HUMBLE GOING TO MY DAD OR GRANDFATHER THAN I WAS WHEN PRAYING TO THE CREATOR OF THE UNIVERSE?! So often I get caught up in God's mercy and love without realizing that He doesn't fool around. He gives you what you deserve along with his mercy and love. Consequences don't disappear when you repent! Did I really think that my earthly father was more powerful than my heavenly one!? How often do I make that mistake?!

God could literally strike you dead in an instant. He's done it before! I'm not saying He will, but you get what I mean. Our hearts need to be humbled before every prayer and *we need to realize the severity of our sins before we so easily accept His grace.* Think about the times you pray. Is it only when something bad happens? Also, think about how the world asks for prayer when a tragedy happens, but wants to remove prayer in schools.

You're basically doing the same thing when you pray only during a tragedy. *Praying should be like breathing.* You should talk to God so often that it becomes habit and eventually becomes natural. You need air to breath. You need God to live.

Thank you Father, for being the breath in my lungs and the joy on my lips. All glory and honor to your name, Lord Jesus. Thank you for your ever present love for me.

1 Thessalonians 2:20

Use the space below to write a prayer that is on your heart:

LISTEN!!

To those who think they are so cool and keep to themselves if they aren't around people who are like them.

LISTEN.

To those who don't look twice when they see someone sitting alone because they can't relate to that person.

LISTEN.

To those who don't talk to someone who is not as pretty or handsome as they think they are.

LISTEN.

Be honest with yourself while reading this. Honesty will benefit you.

Yesterday I was listening to a podcast about loving your neighbor. We all know the verse (Matthew 22: 36-40), but do we have the right idea about it? It is easier to love people similar to you but more difficult to love those who are different. Yes, but what exactly do you define as different? My definition was always those in poverty or the poor or lacking something. I could easily find love for them, so I thought I had loving my neighbor under control, *until today.*

I sat outside my English class, and a girl I had always thought was kinda weird struck up a convo with me about my recent move to the area. She asked if I had made many friends here, and when I said not too many, but a few, she offered to put her number in my phone. I let her, but I didn't think I'd use it. Later, I was sitting with headphones at a table in the cafeteria, doing some homework, when a girl asked if she could sit with me. There were many available tables, and mine was in the corner, so it struck me as odd that she wanted to sit at MY table with ME. I kept the headphones in for a sec, then remembered the message I had heard. SHE was my neighbor I needed to show love to— AND the girl from English!! Neither of these girls seemed to have anything in common with me and, honestly, I was pretty freaked out. With Haley (the girl from English), it seemed like she was genuinely there to listen. With Rachel (lunch girl) it seemed like she needed to be listened to. I had been too prideful to consider becoming friends with either girls, but I was knocked off my high horse very quickly, realizing my neglect to them and girls like them. I can love any high school student, but what about those my age? What about the girls who need to be heard, who are all around me? Remember when I was so worried about making friends? BOOM. Two. Right there. Today. AMEN.

May we pour ourselves into the lives of others with inspiration from Christ and His love.

Thank you, Jesus, for placing people in our lives so we can glorify you and share your love and grace with others. I pray that I am equipped with the armor of God to love and encourage those around me!

Job 13:6

OBEDIENT THOUGHTS

Have you ever cursed someone in your mind? Or wished something bad upon them? An ex? A co-worker? Your boss? Your friend or someone who has wronged you? I HAVEEEEE!!!! So, I turned to a devotional about mercy. I've heard about not forgiving someone and how you are the prisoner when you don't forgive, which is TRUE, but my devotional was about mercy and patience. About how God is so patient with us and yet we think we have the right not to be patient with others. I read this and was slapped right in the face. Why do I think these things? No one is being hurt by these thoughts except me. Where is my merciful heart in praying for people and being an example of God's love!? I know these were thoughts not actions, but they affect me the same. Where is my patience? Maybe God is protecting me from something or helping me learn patience in this way? THEN I read a verse my cousin sent me - 2 Corinthians 10:5: "Take captive every thought and make it obedient to Christ." How convenient that she sent that to me today! God has the craziest ways to show me something after He's told me over and over, and I just don't listen. Think about someone you may not be forgiving or someone you need to show mercy and patience. Pray for them. Pray multiple times if you have to. Every time they enter your mind or you feel the slightest bit of anger. Let's make our thoughts obedient to Christ.

Like 2 Corinthians 10:5 says, I want to take every thought captive, Lord. Thank you for your glory and peace. I pray for strength and obedience as I take every thought captive in order to truly honor and glorify you!

2 Corinthians 10:5

HYPOCRISY

I remember telling everyone about him. After he kissed me I fell so hard. I told everyone how wonderful he was. They would smile with me and watch me blush at his name and squeal through the details of the night of our first kiss. I remember Mrs. Salli, my voice coach, saying, "So y'all are dating now? Or going to?" I hadn't thought that he might have kissed me with no intentions of dating me. I replied with, "I hope so! We are talking about it," just to make it look good, but the truth is, it looked really bad that a woman of God (me) let a man of God (him) kiss her with intentions that were unclear. I know kids my age do that all the time. But it's different when you're children of the Lord called to lead by example and make disciples of men. Jesus didn't put up with hypocrites and that's exactly what I was being when I told the girls I mentor not to kiss a boy before dating. Just because I really liked him didn't mean I should be kissing him outside of a relationship. And just because he seemed flawless in every way didn't mean God put us together in His plan for my future. To some of you I may sound a little extreme, but isn't that what God wants us to be? Extreme obedience to Him is a privilege and a blessing in and of itself. I dare you to examine yourself. I dare you to be completely honest and look at where God wants you to be obedient. And I dare you to surrender in extreme obedience. Not saying it's easy. Just saying it's worth it.

Lord, thank you for strength and self-control. Because I am a child of yours, I have the authority and power to be obedient and honor you. It's a delight to be a child of the King. I want to lead by example and am ready to surrender myself to your perfect Will.

1 Peter 1:14

UM ... THAT'S PERSONAL!

Matthew 5:8: "Blessed are the pure in heart, for they shall see God."

Have you ever been hurt and didn't want advice about it? You needed someone to listen, not to say anything and just listen. I've been there. I was actually there on February 10, 2010. How do I remember this? (It was in my journal, hehe!) Anyway, I read a devotion that was comforting at that time. We often think of God as This Big Being above us who is watching us all the time, and those thoughts can be more scary than comforting. Sometimes we feel unworthy, although we aren't. But because we think that, we try to keep Him at arm's length. IT WILL NOT BENEFIT US to pretend He isn't there when we mess up or feel so guilty or unworthy that we "avoid" Him. Take comfort in being PERSONAL with God. In the darkness He will be your light. Yield your WHOLE being to Him. Do not look to people to tell you about Him, Look to Him directly and He will reveal Himself in a personal way, in ways no other could. On February 10, 2010 I kept God at arm's length and wanted someone to listen. So I sat and talked to my friends, and they gave me encouraging words, but that's not when I felt 100% better. It wasn't until I personally picked up my Bible and got into the Word, that I knew everything would be alright because of God PERSONALLY telling me this through His written Word. To God, we are never one of many. Our sins are not covered, they are WASHED AWAY! They are not only forgiven, but forgotten! Can I get an AMEN!? I pray you hang out with God today and be personal with Him. Honest and personal. Unworthy and broken. Find healing in Him today.

Father, thank you for your listening ears and wide open arms, even when I try to keep you at arm's length. Thank you for your constant pursuit of me and

Ainsley B.

my heart. I'm so thankful to serve a God that puts up with my stubborn nature and loves me beyond my understanding. I pray for comfort and joy in the storm.
   Matthew 5:8

Write a love note to God in the space below:

DON'T HATE ME CUZ
I'M BEAUTIFUL ;)

A friend of mine told me the other day that she felt she doesn't love others as much as she wants to because she doesn't really love herself. It's funny because I used to feel the exact same way. I guess it's not that funny, but it's interesting, because I never realized that was why I wasn't as loving toward others as I wanted to be. I used to pray "Lord, PLEASE allow me to love this person and show your glory through me." Negative thoughts would flood my mind about someone. I didn't want the thoughts to be there, but they were. I wanted to love that person and wanted to be there for them and show them the love of Christ. But for some unknown reason, I couldn't. Over the years, I've noticed a change in my attitude, and I'm extremely thankful, but I didn't realize that the change wasn't so much God changing my heart to love them, but rather changing my heart to love myself, and in turn loving them.

Mark 12:31: "The second is this: 'Love your neighbor as yourself.' There is no commandment greater than these."

I have always looked at this verse and thought it was merely about loving your neighbors, which it is! But it's more than that. The "as yourself" part stuck out to me as I was reading it the other day, and it sent me to a self-discovery moment that brought me to tears.

I treated other people poorly because I didn't love myself. I couldn't look in the mirror without being disappointed in something. I've come to find out that these feelings are more common than I thought with girls. It's so easy to tear ourselves down to try and fit the mold of this world, but if you want to truly love others, you HAVE TO LOVE YOURSELF. The verse says to love your neighbors AS YOURSELF. Hmm … If I don't love myself, how then, will my love look to my neighbors?

The hardest thing for me, believe it or not, was to love my family to such a degree. They know me so deeply and so truly, that I felt TOO comfortable with them and was always rude and disrespectful. Lately, I've taken a step back and gotten to know myself a little better and recognized my pain and loneliness. It's been so beneficial and rewarding that I get overwhelmed with how thankful I am to have my family and that they have put up with me for so long. Here are a few things I did to learn to love myself:

1. Accepted my physical appearance for what it is, rather than what the world wants it to be. Don't get me wrong, I do try to stay in shape, but I used to be so concerned with it that it affected my love for myself. Now, it's just about being healthy. Allow yourself to feel beautiful and stop comparing yourself to others.

2. I became vulnerable and honest with myself. I broke down one night crying (which is very rare) calling out to God, "I don't even know why I'm crying!! I just need help! I don't even know what I need help with! Just help!" It was the most honest, intimate prayer I've prayed in a while. I encourage you to be honest too. No one knows you better than the One who created you.

3. Read *"Captivating: Unveiling the Mystery of a Woman's Soul"* by John and Stasi Eldredge. I know this may affect everyone differently, but it honestly helped me keep promises to myself and stand strong in my beliefs even when people everyone around me didn't share the same beliefs. I became so brave, that I went to church alone! That's a big step for me—don't judge.

A HUGE realization I gained from this book was to truly understand where this hatred for beauty and the emphasis on beauty comes from, and why it was so important to understand where they come from. They come from Satan. Obvious answer, yes, but hear me out. Satan chose Eve to tempt into sin in the garden. Why didn't he choose Adam? Because

Satan was once a beautiful angel. Pride made him fall, so now his revenge is to assault beauty. Eve was beautiful, so he wanted to destroy her. She was glorious, and one with God. What an amazing thing to think about! Girls so often think that they deserve whatever bad thing is happening because of something they have done. Satan tells you that because you are GLORIOUS and a threat to the kingdom of darkness when you shine the light of Christ. Satan attacks because of your beauty and power. Put your guilt away in thinking that you did something to deserve this pain and soak up the fact that you are beautiful and glorious. LOVE YOURSELF, so that you may in turn LOVE OTHERS.

Father, thank you for self-love and encouragement! Bless me with eyes with your vision so I may see myself through your lens of love. I pray for assurance and confidence every day, and I need you with me to walk through such a journey of self-discovery and love. I pray for joy and excitement through such a season, and I glorify your name!

EYE OF THE TIGER!

I walked in to my grandparent's room and found my grandfather watching "Rocky." Incredible movie to anyone, but to him in particular. I can't imagine how he feels. See, he was once an undefeated boxer who was asked, at one point, to go to the Olympics … Do I need to repeat that? Because the first time I heard it, I felt like someone had knocked the wind out of me and installed confusion into my brain. THE OLYMPICS? Yes.. SO why don't we have a reality show and millions of dollars flowing out of our ears? Because he didn't go. His mom asked him not to train for the Olympics and to stay home, so he obeyed. This sent another wave of disbelief to smack me in the face until I thought about it deeper. See, when God allowed this huge opportunity to present itself to my Poppa, the Lord knew what would happen. Many times in my life a really cool opportunity presents itself and it looks so good on the outside, but if I were to take it, I'd be stepping out of God's plan for my life. The Lord allowed this to happen because He knew my Poppa would be obedient and listen to God's plan rather than just what looked good. Poppa now has a loving family, wealth, and happiness. These things may not have happened if he had gone to the Olympics. I MAY NOT BE ALIVE! So it's safe to say it was worth it ;) but really, I still want a reality show.

I encourage you to make every decision carefully. Pray without ceasing before making a final decision and do not step out of God's umbrella of protection.

He is perfectly orchestrating your life; to disobey would only ruin the most beautiful melody of your rhythm called life.

Thank you for your perfect orchestration and plan for my life, Jesus. You go before me and prepare the way, which I am so thankful for. When I try to take the pen and write my own story, it's never as sweet as when you do. Prepare me for the next season in my life and allow me to feel your hand in mine every moment. Thank you for everything you do for your children.

Ephesians 1:3-14

JESUS & JOHN HUGHES

I just was thinking how every girl wants their love story to be like a movie but why on earth do we equate a good love story to a movie? All the lame chick flicks I've seen have heartbreak before happiness in various forms, and it just gets old to me. I'd rather not break up and get back together with someone a million times before deciding they are the one—right? The Creator of the universe is writing my love story and I sometimes wish it was John Hughes (director of *Sixteen Candles*, *The Breakfast Club*, etc) that was directing it?? Geez. I'm dumb from time to time. Trust in the Lord with all your heart and lean not on your own understanding. So, future husband, I'm trusting God has a perfect story for us, but don't hesitate to take me riding on a lawnmower or stand outside my window with a boom box. Just sayin.

Lord, thank you for love and laughter and for my future spouse. I pray today that I honor them and you cover them in protection and love. Thank you for writing my love story and making it perfect in every way. Forgive me for forgetting your perfect plan and wanting to take control of the outcome. I know you will guide and protect me. I love you, Father!

Proverbs 3:5

REMINDER FOR MY GIRLS

Girls,

When you feel like hope is lost, when loneliness sets in, and when impatience seems to be the only way - be strong. Find your strength in the Lord and pursue Him more than ever. I know the desire to be loved and love in return can be overwhelming and painful at times, but the more you fall in love with Jesus, the more fulfilled you will be. No human male can satisfy the desires of your heart more than your Creator, your Father.

I know it's hard to believe and I know it's hard to stay persistent and trust 100% but take advantage of the singleness you've been blessed with! No husband to tend to, no kids to care for, just your relationship with Christ to tend to and rest in. You are SO incredibly loved. SO SO SO loved. Return to the Lord and allow Him to fill your heart with Himself and His amazing joy.

God is fashioning you for your appointed husband, but when you're caught up in haste to find that person, you can't grow to your full potential for your husband or yourself. Be a living example to those around you and show them where true joy comes from. yeah?

Proverbs 3:5-6 (NIV)
Trust in the LORD with all your heart
and lean not on your own understanding;
in all your ways submit to him,
and he will make your paths straight.[a

Father, forgive my haste that is grounded in fear of the future
and fear of the unknown. Create in me a patient heart and

a love for you that burns so brightly no one can deny that it's Jesus who holds my heart. I want to constantly grow in you as you constantly pursue me. Thank you for loving me and tending to my heart.

ROLLING STONES WERE RIGHT ...

"You can't always get what you want, but if you try sometimes you just might find, you get what you need." ("You Can't always Get What You Want" Rolling Stones 1969)

Sometimes you can't do what you want to do. Sometimes you can't date a certain guy if you want your heart to stay pure in Christ. I'm not saying you're better than them, but if they are a temptation (whether it's loving immaturely or physical) you have to say no. it's hard because some people are just so loveable and fun, but if they do not lead you on a righteous path and encourage you in the wisdom of the Lord, it's not right. Self-control is probably the most annoying thing. It's accomplice, "conscience," is also quite annoying. But, the Lord knows His plans for you, and they aren't to send someone in your life to bring you down. Date with your future husband in mind. If a guy gets mad at you for not holding his hand or kissing you on your first date, he's probably not good for you. The Lord will reward your good deeds though. Trust. Trusting is not easy, but it's beneficial in the end. I'd rather miss out on an immature relationship than wake up regretting a simple kiss, and knowing myself, I'd beat myself up for it. Date with your future husband in mind.

"Rest in Me. WAIT upon Me. Seek Me and my fellowship" - God

Thank you, Lord, for your provision and wisdom. I pray for protection over my heart and that I receive what I need and not just what I want. I don't always know what's best for me, Lord. Thank you for knowing my heart and preparing my future relationship. You're the best, God!

Romans 8:25

ARMS WIDE OPEN!!

(while reading this, please turn on Misty Edwards "Arms Wide Open" song)

For God so loved the world that he gave his one and only Son, that whoever believes in him shall not perish but have eternal life.

John 3:16

This is how we know what love is: Jesus Christ laid down his life for us. And we ought to lay down our lives for our brothers and sisters.

1 John 3:16

Interesting, yeah?

Maybe I'm the only one intrigued by this, but to me, that's the Bible slapping me in the face. Everyone knows John 3:16, but the command portion is found in a verse in 1 John. We've heard "love your brothers and sisters ..." but what bothers me is that recently I've been seeing my friends and strangers all about going to different nations to spread God's love (which is incredible, keep it up!) but when it comes to those immediate to them, such as their real siblings or just people in their classes, it's different. I'm not saying I'm not guilty of this and I'm also not saying that everyone does it. I've just noticed how quick we are to judge others around us instead of love them, as if their hearts are any different than those overseas. The physical needs may be different, but look at the hearts of those around you. They are the hardest to love in my opinion. Of course our "brothers and sisters" are those near AND far, but let me put this in context. I have a brother and sisters. I also have sorority sisters as well as my best friends who are like brothers and sisters to me. Sometimes, I don't want to love on them. One of my (family) sisters right now is mad at me for a reason I'm not quite sure of and a part of me wants to give up on her, but I never will. I feel like if she were anyone else, any stranger or kid overseas that I shared the Gospel with, I'd have all the patience in the world, so why not with my sister? Or with my sorority sisters, I hear very little gossip, which I'm thankful for, but nonetheless when you put girls together and mix them up and slap a title on their chests, gossip will come, to some degree. It's super hard for me to be like "hey let's talk about Jesus instead" - but if I were with people I didn't know, I probably would be more comfortable just spilling my guts about my love for the Lord and, more importantly, His love for me. It hurts my heart to experience this, and it hurts my heart even more for those who are blinded to how much they aren't loving others or being loved in return. Giving someone the feeling of being heard and loved is worth more than any check I can write. It may cause sacrifice and it may cause putting your life on hold, but THAT is what we are called to do. I am so convicted of this. I volunteer at a local family homeless shelter, which I love doing, and I can continue to do so, but I struggle to be content knowing I'm not holding my real sister's hand or talking with one of my sorority sisters.

Lord, create in me a willing heart to serve and love with no limit. I need your power for this, because my human nature is not capable. Father, move in my life and make me your hands and feet to those near and far. I pray for my brothers and sisters that they may see YOU instead of me. Jesus laid down his life for us, this is how we know what love is. Teach me to show others what love is by laying down my own life. Amen.

BOYS WILL BE GIRLS, UNLESS …

If I had to describe how conversations with my friend Gennifer make me feel, I'd say something about a breath of fresh air and feeling my DIY feather headdress blowing in the wind on a beautiful day. If you don't know how to take that, it's a good thing. A really refreshing, freeing, good thing. Gennifer is awesome.

We were just chatting about boys (duh) and how girls just don't let boys be boys anymore.

Girls complain "Ohhh my boyfriend won't watch chick flicks with me" or "He spends all his time watching football and doing stupid things outside with his friends" or whatever it may be. Boys are SUPPOSED to swing on trees and break limbs and all that nonsense. We are still young! Let them be men and don't try to control them by trying to take their masculinity away by making them hold your purse! If he wants to play Call of Duty MW3 for an hour of his life, is that really something to get mad about? Sure we could argue if it's affecting his productivity, but nonetheless, it satisfies his feeling of manliness in some sort of way. Do I understand it? Not exactly, but he doesn't understand your shopping addiction either. Can boys still be swinging from trees like monkeys and still be gentlemen? YES. We always think we have to "train" them to be gentlemen. Isn't that what his mom was/is for? We aren't their mothers, and if he isn't a gentleman, then why are you dating him?

Biblically, the men were fighting lions and breaking down pillars and fishing and all that stuff, so why do we insist on taking them to the mall to shop for a cute dress or shoes? No idea, but they are usually miserable with the idea.

Therefore, I give my useless permission to all boys/guys/men: climb trees, build and break things, pretend to be teenage mutant ninja turtles, make up your own crazy games and invent sports. PLEASE. We don't want girly men!

I always get confused when girl's boyfriends are the only person they hang out with. He's your BOYfriend for a reason. let him be a BOY and hang with your GIRLS when you wanna go shopping or talk about the stuff you know that your boyfriend could care less about.

Father, thank you for creating your children so unique and different, and thank you for wild spirits and tender hearts. Thank you also for accepting my rants about random things. I love being a child of God and appreciate the ability to come boldly to the throne to communicate with you :).

Deuteronomy 31:6

LESSON LEARNED

"..spur one another on to good works …"

If you have friends who encourage you with the Word of God and uphold you to a standard and keep you accountable, praise the Lord.

That is so precious and so rare. I'm so so thankful for my friends who I can come to broken and in pain and know they will show me the hope and joy of Christ through their friendship.

If you have friends that tear you down or gossip about you or treat you poorly, don't be afraid to end those relationships. Why would you want to be friends with someone who doesn't care about your well-being or your relationship with Christ?

I learned my lesson a couple of years ago. Since then I have been stronger and I have grown because of the people I surround myself with. Even if I'm far away from the ones at home, I don't replace them with less than phenomenal friends just because I may want quantity over quality.

Choose quality over quantity in your friendship. Be bold for the throne and ultimately for yourself and your heart.

Thank you Father for friends who know and love you more than me and can encourage me and love me and I can love them through you and with you. I'm so blessed.

Thank you, Father, for friends who know and love you more than me and can encourage me and love me so I can love them through you and with you. I'm so blessed.

Hebrews 10:24

JUST THINKING

I was just thinking.

The people we meet, the people we know and the people we love are so interesting. I mean the fact that we know them is interesting. Encounters, relationships, and brief laughs shared with people near to you or far from you—interesting. It just makes me marvel at the Lord's creativity. He knew I needed to know a certain person to understand Him better. He knew I needed to love someone so they could see His love. Isn't it crazy how crucial people in our lives can be? Even if we don't really know them, they can play a huge role. Crazy, right?

Lord, thank you for placing each and every person I know in my path, and I pray that you guide and protect me and those individuals as well. Thank you for your love and sacrifice!

Philemon 1:4

Who are some people in your life that play a unique role? Use the space below to write about them:

MY GOLDEN RULE

Through a string of bad days and heartache, the past few hours have been much, much needed. I woke up with a smile, and that feeling is one of the best ever. I laughed a lot last night and it really is medicine for the soul. My tired, weary soul got exactly what it had been longing for. Jesus really taught me some things I'd needed to learn (like vulnerability) and I'm positive He's not done with me yet. If there's one thing people say to me a lot, it's this: "You have so many friends." YES, I do. I LOVE my friends. Each and every one of them is incredible and I can't even imagine what great things they will accomplish, but I don't think of it as me being their friend because I feel like they do more for me than I could ever do for them, despite my efforts. I feel honored that they let me into their lives. Maybe I'm just close enough to get a glimpse of their lives through the window, maybe they've invited me in for tea, perhaps a slumber party, or maybe we've gotten so close that we are practically roommates. Whatever the closeness may be, I'm honored to have each of them. They are incredible and if I could list them right now I would, but more important than the number is the philosophy I've recently heard and held on to in regards to relationships. My tall friend Andrew, who I call Stretch, told me, "In a relationship, you're to constantly strive to leave the person better than you found them, whether that's over a number of years, months, days, or hours." This was relative to a romantic relationship, but I decided it applies to every relationship you have in life. If you constantly had that mindset, to leave someone better than you found them, with everyone in your life, that could make the biggest difference of all. What does that look like? Encouragement. A tuned ear. A willingness to serve. A sympathetic heart. Whatever their love language is. The more you try to leave people better than you found them, the more you might find the "numbers" grow but become less important than the true treasure of the lives you're honored to be a part of. I've decided it's my new golden rule, to leave people better than I found them. I just look at girls and how they treat each other and see how badly they want true, lasting friendships and I've found that my closest friends constantly make me a better person.

Thank you for community and for wonderful, encouraging people around me, Lord! I pray that I am that for them just as they are for me. I pray for a continued overflow of love and appreciation for those in my life. Thank you thank you!

Matthew 18:20

SELF RESPECT

Look, most boys don't know or understand how fragile girls are, how much we read into things, how much communication we need so we don't feel rejected, how much care they should have with us. They just don't know. That's why it's so important to guard your heart. You have to know your worth and how to love yourself or you'll find yourself so into a guy and with him not knowing how to handle your emotions, you'll end up hurt. There's nothing wrong with caring for a guy or even dating (just in my opinion), but as far as letting someone care for your heart, let Jesus handle that. He's the only one that won't drop it.

Lord, I pray specifically over the heart of this precious reader right now!
Proverbs 4:23

LOVE

When you fall in love, tis a joyous occasion. Your friends and family want to meet this person and everyone wants to know how you met— your story. There's actually a lot of pressure on the story, isn't there? If you met online, people may scoff, or at a bar, some judgement may fall on you. Everyone wants to hear about how one day you were picking flowers in a meadow and he rode up on a white stallion horse and it was love at first sight then y'all rode into the sunset. I'm so guilty of wanting a great story. Not just of love, but of life in general. I want to be able to tell my future kids and grandkids of all sorts of adventures filled with laughter and love, but really, a great story comes with some tears and hardship. A great story comes with empathy with others and walking hand in hand with pain and the thoughts of giving up or quitting and pushing through to prevail! A good story comes from Jesus. Once, I was in a situation where the story was so great— some meadowy flowers and also hardship, lots and lots of hardship. The hardship was like a storm tossing my ship so hard that I lost myself at sea (so to speak). But I didn't remove myself from the situation, why? Because it was a great story. INSANE, right? I thought, "But the story is too good for this situation to not be right." Now I look back and thank God for pulling me out of the boat all together because I've grown and learned and it's created an even better story—a ministry. I can speak to people and truly, truly empathize because I can identify with a lot of struggles through this one situation, and I'm so incredibly thankful that I went through that. But the Lord doesn't want us to be focused on the story—He wants us to trust Him with the story. The less we try to write our own, the better hands we will be in. I'm not sure if any of this makes sense, but it was on my brain this morning.

Lord, take the pen from my hands and write my story as I look to you and you alone. Amennnnnn.

Exodus 14:22

ROLLERCOASTER

I was just thinking about the Christian walk and how often I beat myself up for feeling like I have a "roller coaster" relationship with Christ. One day I'm all butterflies in my tummy high and happy and the next I'm making sure I don't puke on the sharp turns and upside downy loops. Then I was thinking about the word "relationship" and how most if not all of the relationships in my life aren't all easy breezy. There's some push and pull and highs and lows with anyone and everyone, really. From best friend to stranger I, personally, am never at an awesome pumped incredible level with one person at a consistent 100% of the time. Why? Because relationships of all kinds are work and they take effort. So, my last thought was hmm maybe the roller coaster relationship isn't as bad as it seems, since it seems to be one (of many) aspects in every relationship around me. And let me tell you, I have some pretty incredible people and relationships around me. I'm putting down the boxing gloves and not standing in the fight against myself anymore. Instead, I'll put my hands up with Jesus at the top of the mountain (or, roller coaster) and laugh (or AT LEAST be joyful) through the whole ride. No matter the high, no matter the fear of the steep drop below and no matter the climb back to the top.

Thank you, Jesus, for buckling into this rollercoaster with me.

Hebrews 11:1

YOU & SELF

SOME DAYS ARE EASIER THAN OTHERS, LET'S JUST BE REAL ABOUT THAT

My faith, like most people's, has evolved. For the past five years, I have written a blog about my walk with Jesus. There've been highs, and there've been lows. Some entries are long; some are short. Some are stories, some are prayers, and some are just simple truths to remember. I may ramble at times, but I'm a girl and I can feel a lot of different things at once. This book is partly a journal to Jesus, and it's partly a reminder to myself of my walk in faith. I hope you, Reader, can relate to my walk on some level, but most of all I want you to remember that there is always so much freedom in Jesus.

What are some highlights in your walk with God lately? Use the space below to write about them:

YOU ARE BEAUTIFUL

As a female, I've struggled many times with not feeling pretty. I've wanted to look like this girl, or have hair or a body like that girl. It's so easy for us to fall into the temptation of putting ourselves down and wishing we could change one feature or another, but this does NOTHING for our happiness. God says we are fearfully and wonderfully made (Psalm 139:14). Why are you saying that what God made isn't beautiful enough or good enough? When I thought about what I was saying when I said I didn't feel pretty, I thought, "How dare I say that one of God's creations isn't beautiful!" Just because you look different from someone else doesn't mean you aren't as beautiful. We are all unique, and THAT in itself is beautiful. On top of all this, why are we so concerned with the body and our external features? When a man falls in love with a woman, he doesn't just look on the outside, he looks at her personality and her heart. I'm not saying disregard the outside because our body is the temple of God and we should care for it, but don't focus on that completely. Ask God to continue to make you beautiful on the inside for His glory and praise. In doing this, it's amazing how much happier and more confident you will be! (Proverbs 31:10: Charm is deceitful, and beauty is vain, but a woman who fears the Lord will be praised.). Do you think God is looking on your outside? Nope. He looks at your heart, and who better to try to impress or strive to be great for, than the Lord? (1 Samuel 16:7: But the Lord said to Samuel, "Do not look on his appearance or on the height of his stature, because I have rejected him. For the Lord sees not as man sees: man looks on the outward appearance, but the Lord looks on the heart.") Therefore, praise the Lord for creating you as you are, unique and BEAUTIFUL!

Thank you Lord, for the beauty and grace that you have adorned me with! I'm so thankful for a God that loves my heart and soul and allows me to enjoy the confidence of being a child of the Risen King! Thank you for a beautiful heart. Create in me a love for people so I may pour out your love and beauty to others!

Job 40:10

What are practical ways you can remember your beauty? Use the space below to list some ways:

TO: PRINCESSES EVERYWHERE!

I'm currently reading the book *Captivating: Unveiling the Mystery of a Woman's Soul* by John and Stasi Eldredge and falling in love with the words and discovering my more "feminine" side. I wanted to write about one thing I read because it was profound and really hit home with me.

"I know I'm not alone in this nagging sense of failing to measure up, a feeling of not being good enough AS A WOMAN. Every woman I've ever met feels it- something deeper than just the sense of failing at what she does. An underlying, gut feeling of failing at who SHE IS. *I am not enough,* and *I am too much* at the same time. Not pretty enough, not thin enough, not kind enough, not gracious enough, not disciplined enough, But too emotional, too needy, too sensitive, too strong, too opinionated, too messy. The result is Shame, the universal companion of women. It haunts us, nipping at our heels, feeding on our deepest fear that we will end up abandoned and alone."

If you haven't ever felt the emotions in that paragraph, congrats. Teach me your ways, oh wise one. For those of you who have, I want to encourage you to not feel shame in who you are. It's okay to want to be romanced and feel like a damsel in distress. It's okay to wear sparkly dresses and be afraid of bugs. It's also okay to own boys in Call of Duty or know all the stats of the LSU football team. THAT.IS.BEAUTIFUL.

YOU.ARE.BEAUTIFUL.

Look at yourself in the mirror. But, before that, pray that God shows you what He sees through HIS eyes. This means you won't see your large lumpy butt or your rib cage poking from your thin frame, it means you'll get a glimpse of your HEART.

Enough with the "I'm not good enough" or the "I'm too much to handle" - EMBRACE BEING A WOMAN and love being you. Love the quirks that only you have. Stop being embarrassed by the little things. It's important to be comfortable in yourself to be able to grow and mature in the Lord and to see the true beauty in all women.

You're captivating.

Jesus, thank you for creating each one of your children so unique and wonderful! Thank you for the little winks you give us every day to remind us that you love us and are with us! I pray for confidence and boldness to walk in my true identity and joyful spirit!

John 1:12

I AM NOT NAKED!

Remember the time a rumor was spread about you? Or the shame you felt when someone made fun of you for whatever reason? You're not pretty enough. You're too fat. You're not as cool as they are because they do this and you do that. You're too much to handle. Too different. Remember when you didn't want to do something because you feared what others would say? Too shamed to stand up for yourself or what you believe? When did you hide in the bushes as Adam and Eve did after they ate of the forbidden fruit due to shame and worry?

When did someone strip you of your pride and leave you naked?

A little girl ran up to her mom crying her eyes out. When her mom asked what was wrong she replied, "They said I was ugly!" Her mom stood up with rage in her eyes to look around at who might have wounded such a fragile little heart and bent down to eye level of her daughter and asked, "WHO TOLD YOU THAT YOU WERE UGLY?"

Every day we are told or tell ourselves another lie, just as Satan told Adam and Eve when he tempted them with the fruit. They ate of it and hid from God. God spoke, "Where are you?" Adam replied that he had heard God walking in the Garden and was afraid because he was naked so he hid. God spoke again, "WHO TOLD YOU THAT YOU WERE NAKED?" Who told you such a lie and wounded your fragile heart?

Who told you that you're ugly?

Who told you that your dream was too big?

Who told you that you are too tall or too short?

WHO TOLD YOU THAT YOU ARE NAKED?

… that you won't amount to anything … that you're worthless …

He asks you this question in order to reveal the lie in it. In Christ, WE ARE NOT NAKED. He's covered us.

Isaiah 61:10

I delight greatly in the LORD;

my soul rejoices in my God.

For he has clothed me with garments of salvation

and arrayed me in a robe of his righteousness,

as a bridegroom adorns his head like a priest,

and as a bride adorns herself with her jewels

so what now? What do you do with what you just read?

Believe the unbelievable.

Grace.

the Gospel.

Christ.

Love.

Beauty.

Hopes.

Dreams.

BELIEVE IN YOURSELF.

Come to the Father humble, sick, broken, and BEAUTIFUL.

Father, thank you for grace, dreams, love, and hope. Remind me how loved I am and how much you care, Lord, Remind me how treasured I am in your eyes, how valued and glorified. Thank you for loving me at my worse and rejoicing with me at my best. I love you.

Isaiah 61:10

Whew, that was a long one.. thoughts? Use the space below for brain spills:

LAWD HAVE MERCY!

I've always wished there was a magical memory eraser wand where you'd think about what memory you want to erase from someone else's mind, and BiPpItY bOpPiTy BoOm, it would be gone. (Not from your mind though, because you have to remember not to say or do whatever it was again and repeat history). Maybe it'd look like a plunger, a sparkly one, of course. ANYWAY basically I just wish there were some things I didn't have to experience to learn. But in church this morning one word stuck out to me. Mercy. I take advantage of, cry in thanksgiving for, and don't deserve God's loving mercy. When I heard that one word, I thought to myself, "God is so good to give His mercy so wonderfully. I wish people were more like that." Then I went back to listening. Later, walking out of church I got in my car and felt like this question was written on my windshield it was so obvious, "DO YOU SHOW ENOUGH MERCY TO OTHERS?" We, as Christians, pray for people around us to change or have a huge God experience or something, then they do and we aren't willing to extend mercy and accept their change. We become skeptical and as soon as we see them stumble in some form or fashion we say, "Oh I knew it. I knew his change wasn't real." BOOM. There's the moment. That's the thought that needs to be erased or reconstructed to sound like "Oh, they need support. I'm gonna go talk with them and see how I can help their transformation," because transformation is not a destination, IT'S A PROCESS. That is sooooo easily forgotten and overlooked. We think that we are climbing a rock wall to ring the bell at the top. Well, that rock wall doesn't have a bell at the top. You keep climbing and climbing and sometimes you slip, but the merciful and serving hearts and support of whoever is holding you - community, family, church, or God alone - step in and keep you going. It's hard. It may cause blisters or scars, but it's worth it to further the kingdom of God. So WORTH IT. We are called to be like Christ. For the sake of not writing a novel, I just want the word MERCY to stand out right now. You don't know everything that other people have been through, extend mercy today. I'm working on that too. Will you help me be more merciful? Will you be merciful to me?

-Jude 1:22-23

-Matthew 5:7

Exodus 7:20 Moses and Aaron did just as the LORD had commanded. He raised his staff in the presence of Pharaoh and his officials and struck the water of the Nile, and all the water was changed into blood.

Lord, Thank you for your constant mercy. Equip me to extend the same to my peers and fellow brothers and sisters in you. You paid the price for me and the least I can do is extend a merciful hand and heart. Help me remember that and to provide unconditional love to those around me. Thank you Jesus!

SOMETIMES I LIKE MY FORGETFULNESS ...

Burdened with memories today. I wish I was as forgetful about those sometimes as I am everything else in life. Where is my phone? When is that project due? Who did I mistakenly give my heart to that time? HA!

Ever have days like that?

It's not easy walking with the Lord and picking up your Cross daily. Sometimes you don't even wanna acknowledge that your cross is there at all ... I used to allow myself days to wallow in self-pity haha what a mistake! I did that until one day my friend DJ said "If you don't choose joy, you won't find joy ... choose joy over sadness every time" boom, never choosing sadness again!

But imagine if God had that attitude of not wanting to deal with us or acknowledge that we were on the earth ... I'm terrified to know what my life would be like if one day He cared and the next He just didn't feel like it.

Thank you Father for your love and kindness and mercy. I would be more lost than ever without His grace and goodness.

Choose joy today.

Thank you, Father, for your love and kindness and mercy. I would be more lost than ever without your grace and goodness.

2 Timothy 1:9

GIRLY GIRRRRRRL!

The other day I saw a tweet that began with, "Forgive me for being such a girl, but ..." and I immediately thought, "Why do you think that you have to be forgiven for acting like a girl as if it's a bad thing?" I'm just so confused as to why we don't let boys be boys or girls be girls. UMMM ... no. I'm a girl. I like getting my nails done and being pretty and dressing up and wearing glitter and planning my future life with my future husband and our future children and I'M NOT ASHAMED OF IT! I like PINK! (it's not my absolute favorite, but hey, I still like it!) I like to giggle and wear heels! Who are these people that are trying to prevent girls from being girls and if no one, then why do girls feel like they are being persecuted for things they like? I cry during sad movies and I bake like a champ, so if a guy asks me to make him a sandwich (politely), it'll be the best sandwich he's ever had! (if it's in a disrespectful manner it'll be the best knuckle sandwich he ever had!)

Be you. Don't let anyone tell you that who you are isn't okay. Jesus made you as you are. Embrace it and glorify Him through your strengths. Don't try to manipulate yourself for everyone around you, especially a boy.

Lord, Thank you for creating me a daughter of the Risen King. Thank you for the passion and heart you've put inside of me and for allowing me to walk in in your Will. I pray for all of your daughters that we embrace and enjoy being women and children of God, pursuing your Will for us and inspiring those around us! Thank you for knowing our hearts and loving us through anything and everything!

Proverbs 31:26

RUNNING MY RACE

. . . .

I think selfishness drives disobedience.

Impatience.

Fear.

along with many other emotions that cut like rusted metal to the heart.

Sometimes I get frustrated if I fall into a sin or temptation because I'm supposed to be a child of God, which means I mess up less than the average human, right?

I'm a Christian. I am THE example. I have to do the right thing. ALWAYS or I'll be struck by lightning. right?

wrong.

This morning I felt overwhelmed by the Spirit along with a trillion other emotions, mostly happy, but my heart felt a little heavy.

I've heard the "Christians aren't perfect" sermon more than enough times to know that my blog isn't some revolutionary discovery about Christianity, but I need to be reminded not to be so hard on myself sometimes. Sometimes I deserve a punch in the gut by God and He merely gives me a slap on the wrist (praise the Lord for mercy!!!)

If we're being real, I deserve death.

That's scary.

I just think that I have to allow my failures or my slip ups to be a testimony of growth and how we never stop growing as Christians. We are to run the race with endurance, and it's not just a half-marathon race like I often try to make it. I trip and fall in the race, but my Father is right beside me encouraging me, thus preparing me to encourage others. My selfishness causes me to stumble, but mercy keeps me humble.

I am thanking the Lord for trials and failures, because I run closer to Him each time. Sometimes I take two steps back, but usually it causes four forward when I realize my humanness.

I'm not perfect. I'm a walking testimony of why I/we need Christ so much.

Thank you Father for mercy, lessons and opening my eyes and reminding me of the importance of my relationship with you.

Thank you, Father, for mercy, for lessons, and for opening my eyes and reminding me of the importance of my relationship with you.

2 Corinthians 12:8-9

ANGRY BIRD, SAVING GRACE

Sometimes I break down and lose it. Sometimes I cry out of fear, guilt, pain, etc. This happens less than it did two/three years ago, thanks to Jesus, but it still happens from time to time. Sometimes I don't feel like I can make it through whatever I'm dealing with and I feel like it's going to last forever or the pain will at least ... but, I can't always hide it and pretend everything is okay. Why do we think that being a Christian means that we have to live perfect lives and have the right answers to everything? Wisdom doesn't just happen, it comes from learning and growing. I feel like many people assume that Christians are supposed to hurt less or for a smaller amount of time. I WISH!!! But that's simply not true. Of course we have a hope and a love that is unconditional from our Heavenly Father which is beyond my imagination, but we are also human. Humans hurt, cry, grieve, sin, etc. I imagine God FIGHTING for me— FIGHTING the battle that HE took upon his shoulders as He hung from the cross. I don't have to be strong or perfect or wise all the time because my God makes GOOD out of ALL things. It's SO hard to think that good will come out of the hard stuff. That death and break ups and temptations and all that stuff can be molded into a beautiful, GOOD thing. God is GOOD. He is FIGHTING for me and He LOVES me. He knew these times would come before I was even born! I get scared and I get mad and I just want to fall into His arms and be a weak little bird afraid to leave the nest, but He gave us full armor to fight alongside Him in our weakest times. He isn't just beside us, he is INSIDE of us. The greatest warrior lives inside of you. (He's living on the inside roaring like a lion.) Be encouraged through the hard times, the guilt, and the frustration that we serve the God of life and happiness, and even though we get discouraged and beat ourselves up,

He is our strength and ever-present help in trouble. He never leaves. He never forsakes. He turns all the hurt into something good that will glorify HIM! PRAISE!!

I just can't do it alone. Praise the Lord I don't have to.

Lord, thank you for walking with me and reminding me that I'm not alone. I'm so thankful for your passion and love for me and that you are willing to fight for your children. I'm so grateful to be in your army!

Romans 8:37-39

I LOVE MYSELF!

The second biggest thing that breaks my heart is when girls look at their lives through a lens of tragedy. The first is sexual abuse, but the second is when girls talk about being depressed and suicidal when they are in a beautiful home with a loving family, because it's not their circumstance that causes the sadness in their hearts, it's what they tell themselves. What you tell yourself has so much power over your life. If I wake up and complain about my life non-stop, I'll start believing that my life isn't as sweet and wonderful as it is. If I wake up with a positive attitude and thank the Lord for my many blessings and live in gratitude, then I won't have such a depressed attitude about myself and my surroundings. When I choose to believe I'm beautiful and worth being a daughter of the King, I can look at my life through a lens of thanksgiving and joy instead of tragedy, looking for hope in false idols. Be positive. Be happy. Be thankful.

I will enter your gates with thanksgiving and praise, Lord God! I want to take a moment today and just thank you for everything you've given me: breath, health, a home, and a warm meal. It's crazy how often I take those things for granted, and I ask for forgiveness and for a reminder of how blessed I truly am. Thank you, Jesus!

Psalm 19:14

PEOPLE CAN'T HEAL YOU

I don't know how many people go through this, but I know a number of girls who've experienced that sad feeling and frustration that comes with it when you're dying for someone to notice. You just want someone to look in your eyes and see that you're upset, and you want them to just see it and know. Here's the thing about that—People aren't mind readers. Here's the bigger thing about that—People can't heal you. So often, people cry out for people, but that's not going to help or heal unless you've cried out to The Lord first and you are merely getting support and accountability from people. Your boyfriend, can't fix it. Even your mom has flaws when it comes to recognizing pain in others because we try to pretend we are hiding it, but begging for someone to notice. This logic never made sense to me as a teen, but now that I've found the Healer, Jesus Christ, it's so clear to me how silly it was to hope for people to notice my sadness when The Lord was here the whole time saying, "run to me. I will save you my child."

Thank you Jesus for your patience and love. Your forgiveness is overwhelming and your mercies are new. Thank you thank you thank you!

Look to Jesus.

Thank you, Jesus, for your patience and love. Your forgiveness is overwhelming and your mercies are new. Thank you thank you thank you!

Psalm 106:1

STRUGGLES

Me: I want to be perfect and skinny with a wonderful boyfriend and straight A's.

Jesus: deny the things that pertain to the outward man in order to perfect the inner life and enrich your knowledge of Me.

Me: but that's so hard :(

Jesus: so was getting beaten and hung on a cross for every sin every committed, including yours.

Me: ... touché.

Please forgive me for my ignorance and human nature. You are my everything, and I need to start acting like it!

2 Corinthians 9:15

Write about a conversation you've had with God lately in the space below:

WRITE IT

Sometimes you just have to repeat this in your head millions of times:

"I am worthy of being pursued. I am beautiful. I will not let a guy define my happiness. I love myself. I love my future husband. Patience is hard, but it'll be worth it. I am a daughter of the King."

words are powerful.

In Jeremiah 29:11 you remind me of your faithfulness and plan for my life. Thank you, Jesus!!

Jeremiah 29:11

What are you telling yourself? Use the space below to write encouraging words to yourself:

YOU'RE BEAUTIFUL

One day you'll decide you're beautiful. That day can be today if you step off the scale and look in your precious, compassionate heart and bury your comparison to the girl beside you. You're beautiful whether you choose to believe it or not, but if there's one thing I've learned, it seems that the more you love yourself, the more you love others and what's better than so much love surrounding one person?

WHY I LOVE SELFIES

I'll be honest, sometimes there are some people who are interesting selfie takers. In a world where people make fun of other people for taking pictures of themselves, I say— go for it!!! Why? Because if you feel beautiful enough in that moment to capture it, then be okay feeling beautiful!! I LOVE when girls feel beautiful and that's become a way to express that so bump everyone who makes fun and go for it. It's okay to feel beautiful! Yes, this post was sparked by a comment made about my newest IG pic of me in a hat I bought yesterday and love, but that's how I feel. I wish more girls loved themselves enough to post all sorts of selfies all the time!

What are your thoughts on selfies? Use the space below to write about them:

CHIN UP, SOLDIER

I don't know what it is, maybe the phone call I got in the middle of the night the other night to pick up a young girl from the hospital, maybe the flood of messages in my inbox asking for help … The realization that teenage girls all around me and all around the world are crying out for help has never been so apparent, and I just can't tell enough people how important it is to tell young girls how much they are loved and to love on them. I remember being in high school and feeling like I was being watched under a microscope and only really feeling love depending on if my crush talked to me or not. HOW WRONG I WAS! Too many girls are fooled by the devil into thinking that they are alone and unloved. That they are the only one cutting, crying, and contemplating too many dangerous things and that no one understands. TRUST ME, people understand. This is not a "you're wrong for feeling the way you do" post because I know so many girls are told that these days. This is a post telling you that there is hope. That it gets better, I promise. That a man can't fulfill your self-worth (in fact, that's the scariest place to put it) and that you're a strong, passionate woman with dreams the size of mountains and determination to climb said mountains. It's possible. The world is at your fingertips if you just look beyond today. Look beyond the gossip and look beyond the glares. I know I know how hard it can be. I know. But GUESS WHAT: OUR GOD IS BIGGER. God can take away any pain and insecurity. He has and He will continue to. I couldn't have written anything like this three years ago. I didn't know that I could feel so loved. I'm not saying "come to Jesus and it will be easy" because it won't. But it is worth it. It's hope, love, joy, and the strength to overcome everything. Every sharp word, every lost relative, every tear and every sorrow. It can ALL be overcome and overlooked. My trick to it is focusing on the positive, confessing to Jesus when I feel weak, allowing myself to feel how I'm feeling, identifying where the feeling came from and then giving it to God. Yes, easier said than done, but so worth it when you've given it over :). I hope, you, the reader, know how loved you are and if you're looking right and left and no one is there, look up. I wish I could hug all of you or have a cup of coffee and hear your heart, but it's simply out of reach, so I hope my electronic hugs and coffee dates serve some sort of positive purpose and I hope you know I love you.

Thank you for a heart for your children, Lord. I pray that I never cease loving them and wanting to improve their well-being, through your love and power. Thank you for choosing me and other like-minded women to love and tend to younger girls. I pray over them right now to feel loved, treasured, and valued!

Proverbs 31:25

ONE THING REMAINS

One thing remains.

One thing remains.

YOUR LOVE NEVER FAILS, IT NEVER GIVES UP, IT NEVER RUNS OUT ON ME.

IT GOES ON AND ON AND ON AND ON IT GOES, FOR IT OVERWHELMS AND SATISFIES MY SOUL!

AND I NEVER EVER HAVE TO BE AFRAID!

("One Thing Remains" by Jesus Culture)

God is not done with you yet and He is with you.

He can handle your anger and pain. YOU can't.

He is healer.

When a child gets hurt physically, blood everywhere and bruised and broken, he doesn't clean it up before taking it to mom or dad. It's messy and ugly and painful.

That's how you come to the Father. No need to clean it up before. Come bloody, broken, and bruised.

Whatever you're going through, God is there. Whether you like it or not, God is there.

Come to Jesus.

Thank you, Lord, for allowing me to come to you broken and distraught and for loving me just the same. I truly can't fathom your love, and I'm so thankful to serve a God who embraces my messiness and loves me unconditionally! Your grace and mercy are overwhelming.

1 Chronicles 16:7-36

WHY ADULTS "DON'T UNDERSTAND"

How many times does "my parents just don't understand" enter your mind? I bet a lot if you're in high school. If you're in college it may be more like "my mom was right the whole time." But back to the lack of understanding part. Young people think that their parents don't understand because parents may not agree with choices or decisions being made by the young person (aka you). I was just thinking about why parents "don't understand" and I think I've figured out at least one reason.

They know better because they've been there. Now, they may all say this, but here's how it really translates (in my brain):

"You shouldn't be out past midnight." = I know what happens in the world (more than you do because you probably don't watch the news) and most of the bad happens in the darkness. I want you safe. And no matter where you are going, you're not invincible.

"You shouldn't call boys." = you deserve to be pursued and boys like a chase, so let him pursue you.

"Don't hang out with that crowd." = you're influenced by the people around you whether you believe it or not. If you don't want to be that gossipy-drama filled girl, don't hang out with her.

"Don't watch rated R movies." = Again, whether you believe it or not, media is constantly surrounding you and you are constantly consuming it. The movies want to make you believe that bad behavior is "normal" or want to put fear in your spirit with scary movies. This is not cool. I'll be transparent here: I don't watch rated R movies if there's nudity in them or other circumstances, depending on my reasoning. I just feel like girls should respect themselves more, and it breaks my heart to know that they think their worth is only physical when it's not.

"Don't wear that short skirt." = modest is hottest. Seriously, leaving more to the imagination is good, especially for guys because they'll see you as the dating/marriage type, not the kiss em and diss em type! And guess what, your parents learned that a long time ago.

So to prevent any more babbling - it's not that parents don't understand it's that they learned the lessons so long ago, that they (sometimes) forget the feelings of not understanding 100% of who you are and what your self-worth is.

They've learned the lessons and want to protect you from learning the hard way and for someone who is still young and without kids, trust me, if you can listen and learn the easy way—do it.

Respect yourself and your parents. I promise, they're smarter than you think.

Thank you for those who have lived this life longer than us and know more things about life in general, Lord. Thank you for placing them in our lives so we may grow in wisdom and understand honor. I pray over parents right now. And I pray you will place a bridge of communication between them and their children because it's so important that parents and children know and understand each other! Thank you, Lord!

Exodus 20:12

TO: YOU

To the girl who looks in the mirror only to see a stranger.
To the girl who feels the scars on her wrists and the urge for new ones.
To the girl who can't seem to lift her spoon or fork.
To the girl who thinks she lifts those too often.
To the girl who cries, wears a disguise and sometimes feels like she wants to die:

1. You should know that my friends and I are praying for you.
2. I'm praying for you by name (if you've contacted me or if I've seen any sort of post or heard of anything).
3. Break the mirror, put down the razor, eat whatever you want, you are NOT fat. YOU ARE BEAUTIFUL, LOVED, and ONE OF A KIND.

Choose every day to love yourself.
Empower yourself.
You're a princess of the King!
Find your self-worth in Jesus and watch His glory be revealed in your life!!
And lastly, Live.

THIS MORNING

I woke up normally this morning, earlier than I wanted but ya know, it happens. And I looked in the mirror and had the typical girl reaction— "ew" And I ran an errand just in my "ew" state, and it wasn't until I got back home and was about to jump in the shower that I realized that every single morning, every single day, every single MOMENT, there is someone who loves me so much, He sees me as flawless, pure, and blameless even in my "Ew."

Every morning I wake up and The Lord says, "Good morning, my beautiful daughter. Put on my armor and take on the world today." Every morning. Every morning I am called worthy and beautiful and receive a new heap of mercies and joy laid upon me and it occurred to me that some mornings and some days, I don't accept it. I don't delight in Him and say, "thank you, more please Father!" I wake up and say, "Ew."

I shall write on my mirror a reminder to change that.

ADVENTURES WITH JESUS

I like imagining adventures. I guess you know that if you have read my post about hiking with Jesus, but today I feel like we are in an airplane. A small one and I'm sitting by the window. As I look out above the millions of trees and tiny bodies of water (we aren't that high, more like a sea plane kinda thing) he says, "I made this for you. I made this so you can look out in awe and wonder at the beauty of nature and get a teeny tiny microscopic glimpse of what happens when I see you. You are worth SO much more than those trees you love. Those animals you get so happy seeing. You are more beautiful than those flowers in the fields and you often don't believe it. You look in the mirror wondering how to "fix" yourself, but I made those flowers so you know that you're ten zillion times more beautiful than they are." I smile and tears fill my eyes as I look out of the window again. His arm around my shoulders he whispers, "Daughter, you will be cared for and grow and blossom as the lilies do. You will be strong and stand tall as the trees and you will be as calm as the still waters beneath us."

Thank you, Father.

Psalm 3:2-6

ADVENTURES WITH JESUS II

Today didn't find me on a hiking trail or in a sea plane overlooking creation. Today ... Today found me at Jesus' feet, weeping in defeat and discouragement. It found me in apologies and sorrow unable to look up at Him, just in the fetal position at His feet, crying out to Him.

He looked down at His beloved, tears filled His eyes as he picked up my chin. He knew everything I felt, everything that made my heart so heavy. He had been holding his hand out, waiting for me to grab it for a while and this was the moment He had known I would have to make it to before I did so. He lifted my chin, held out his hand to help me up and told me to look Him in the eye. He said, "You are mine. Your peace and joy comes from me. Your healing and hope comes when you walk with me. When we are hand in hand." "I don't deserve this grace, Lord. I can't accept it," I would cry. "Ainsley. (If you don't feel a heart squeeze thinking about Jesus calling you by name, whew!) You are MY daughter. MY heart and MY reason for dying on the cross. The exact reason you're weeping at my feet is why I died. You have been forgiven and you WILL accept my grace because I didn't die for you to feel so defeated and lifeless. I died to give you life abundantly and follow through with my promises. The empty promises you've heard from man are NOT an example of my provision and promise for your life. I am the God of the universe and I am FOR you. I am on your team and in your heart. I am the one you find on the trail and in the plane and on any and all other adventures we have been on and will continue to go on. I send angels before you to protect you, Daughter. I am Yours and You are MINE."

I crawled up in His lap and rested my head on His shoulder. Weak and feeble I ran out of tears, but a flood of memories came back to me in that place. The promises, visions, dreams and goals he planted in my heart and in my life. Fear of abandonment, of the future and of so many other things vanished in His presence and I felt my heart in His care and unconditional love. He whispered, "I love you." I whispered back, "I love you too. Thank you Jesus."

My heart can barely handle the love you have for me. Thank you, Father. May I be a vessel for others who have found themselves where I've been, and let my story be a testimony of your greatness!

Daniel 12:3

What's your latest adventure with Jesus? Write about it in the space below:

FEAR ON THE FLOOR

. . . .

I've found myself in a full-fledged melt down consumed in fear of the future. Why am I telling anyone this? I don't know. Because my journal is bruised from all my writing in it and I want to be transparent. I'm literally lying on the ground crying like a child because of a few reasons, but mainly because I'm scared. I'm scared of losing people, not having a loud enough voice for Unveiled for it to be successful, etc. You get it. If you don't know already, Unveiled was birthed from my own struggles. It's a daily battle I personally face thinking "I'm not good enough to love." Or "I'm not smart enough to be successful." Yeah I'm getting real transparent here. Buckle up. Every time I read or hear a story, every time a girl approaches me, sends me a message, tweet, comment, whatever, I want to hug them and just say, "me too." Maybe we don't have the same story, but maybe we have similar lies. I'm one of those "broken home" kids. My parents' divorced when I was young but I always thought it didn't affect me since I was so young and didn't know any different. Until I realized that a fear of abandonment had crept its way into the deepest darkest parts of my heart and it has taken years of self-discovery and unveiling of lies to almost grasp the falseness of that insecurity. But sometimes I'll slap it in the face and sometimes it crawls up beside me and just has the softest hand hold because evil isn't always abrupt. I do smile and believe in Jesus but that doesn't mean I don't cry and wonder why things happen. Not just to me. I cry for everyone who relates to Unveiled. I cry for you who lost a family member or you who just went through a break up. You with the eating disorder, and you who has anxiety. I cry extra for you who don't think life is worth living and want to end it all. I cry a lot, actually. My heart sometimes physically hurts like a brick is being laid on it. I tell you this because I need to vent aaaaaand

118

because I want you to know I can relate. When I speak to audiences (present and future) my heart is so burdened and it's so passionate for you to find healing, but it's also searching for hands to hold so we can all heal together. I know you need to know you aren't alone, and so do I.

I pray for community. I pray for the comfort of belonging, and I rebuke fear and insecurity. Thank you for working miracles in my life, Lord. I am nothing without you. I pray for each heart, near and far. Consume us, Lord! Let us feel your mighty power and love always. Thank you, thank you!!

Micah 4:4

TESTIMONY

I received this letter from a reader and wanted to share it. I love your incredible hearts and exciting journeys!

Hello Ainsley!

My name is Sandra, I'm 16 years old and I'm writing this all the way from Tenerife, Spain (although I'm from Venezuela). So I've followed you for a little over a year and out of all the incredible things I've learnt from you there is one that stands out the most to me. Over the past few years I've had a little bit of a fall into this dark place inside my head, but that's a story for another day, and one of those grey days, sometime in June last year, I stumbled upon a few words on your blog that I've kept with me ever since. "But the story is too good for this situation to not be right." I don't really know what it meant to you in that moment but I know that it meant a lot to me. So much so that I felt the urge to write it down. Those few words are written on the very first page of the little heart-shaped notebook where I capture all the positive thoughts I save for myself. So whenever I'm not feeling my best, that short sentence puts a bright future right before my eyes and it's all because of you, the beautiful girl who decided to share those words. Thank you for that. Thank you for the bunch of other awesome thoughts you've given me to spill on those pages. Thank you for Unveiled. And thank you for everything you continue to do for this mad world. Not a day passes that I don't look up to you. Can't wait to read the incredible book you're putting together. Hearts, rockets and all my best wishes! A million kisses, Sandra.

What is Unveiled?

Unveiled is a campaign that aims to improve self-worth and self-confidence in teens and young adults by "Unveiling" the lies we believe about ourselves. Through media, community and understanding, we hope to communicate helpful tools and resources to remove the "I'm not good enough" in our lives and replace it with "I'm more than enough and I am worthy." To find out more about the campaign and it's latest information, visit <u>UnveiledCampaign.com</u>, follow @unveiledcampaign on Instagram and @Unveiled_camp on Twitter.

To find out more information on how to bring Unveiled to your high school or college, visit <u>AinsleyBritain.com</u> and fill out a contact form.

Thank you

To my family and friends who have supported me through all of my crazy dreams. For this book specifically, my grandmother who was/is always willing to help and asking what she can do to advance my dream. To my wonderful editors who have put up with me through the process of adding, subtracting, grammar mistakes and the list continues. Thank y'all for being so helpful and wonderful! I was hoping to have Louisiana based editors, so when my grandmother told me about Carol and Nancy, Copper Iris Books, I was elated and they go above and beyond expectations! I'm so thankful. To every song, artist, quote & human I referenced or quoted. Thank you for inspiring people, including myself. Being a vessel for the Lord's work is what I aim to be and you've done just that, impacting more lives than just mine!

Madison, I love and miss you, always … no matter what.

Printed in the United States
By Bookmasters